QUICK AND EASY
UPHOLSTERY

QUICK AND EASY
UPHOLSTERY

15 STEP-BY-STEP
EASY-TO-FOLLOW PROJECTS

ALEX LAW • POSY GENTLES

CICO BOOKS
LONDON NEW YORK

Published in 2008 by CICO Books
an imprint of Ryland, Peters & Small Ltd
519 Broadway, 5th Floor
New York NY 10012
Copyright © CICO Books Ltd 2008

Text copyright © Posy Gentles and Alex Law
Photographs copyright © CICO Books 2008

10 9 8 7 6 5 4 3 2 1

A CIP catalog record for this book is available from the Library
of Congress.

ISBN-13: 978 1 906094 46 1
ISBN-10: 1 906096 46 2

Printed in China

Editor Sarah Hoggett
Designer Claire Legemah
Step-by-step photography Debbie Patterson
Style photography Christopher Drake

The authors would like to offer their thanks to:
Alexandra, Rob, Steve, Terry, and Edd for all
their help during the making of this book.
A huge thanks also to Amy, Margaret,
Edmund, William, Frieda, and Minna for
their continued support.

Contents

THE
BASICS

Quick and Easy Upholstery teaches the classic principles of traditional upholstery using natural and sustainable materials—linen, horsehair, burlap, and muslin—to create furniture that you won't find in the stores. This section sets out a few indispensable tools, core materials, and simple techniques, allowing even complete beginners to create stunning and unique pieces. Armed with this information, you will be ready to rescue old and beautiful chairs, beds, and footstools with fabulous new fabrics, or renovate a treasured heirloom in perfect period style.

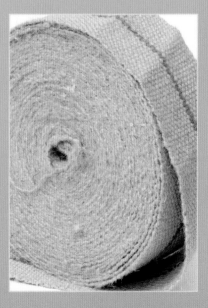

Tools and materials

Using natural materials with their subtle and harmonizing colors, the rich dusty smell of the burlap, the silkiness of linen twine, the lightness of a sack of horsehair, is a singular pleasure of upholstery. There is a sense of tradition as you strip down an antique piece of furniture, knowing that you are renewing it using the same skills and materials that have been used for centuries.

There is a joy, too, in collecting tools that have been refined through the years specifically for the purpose of upholstery. You will probably already have some general-purpose tools—shears and a tape measure, pliers and a mallet—in your toolbox, but you will need to invest in some basic upholsterer's tools.

ORGANIZING A TOOLKIT

As with any discipline or skill, being well organized and making sure that all your tools and materials are close at hand when you need them is half the battle. All too often, that initial flush of enthusiasm that we all have at the start of a project can be seriously dampened by having to take time out to search for a pair of shears or a tape measure. Find a box or a case that you can store your tools in. It's also worth building up a collection of small jars so that you can keep all the different sizes and types of small items, such as tacks and pins.

THE WORK PLACE

Although we may dream of having a workroom all of our own, for most of us it remains a fantasy. The projects in this book have all been designed so that they can be carried out in your kitchen or a spare room. You will need a worksurface—a kitchen table is perfect. Working on the floor will eventually hurt your back and knees. Make sure that the room you're working in has plenty of light and lay out a folded blanket to protect both your work surface and your project. It's also a good idea to put down a dustsheet to catch any roving tacks and dust.

TOOLS FOR STRIPPING

Stripping simply means removing any existing upholstery. It's the first stage in any upholstery renovation project.

PINCERS: FLUSH CUT (small)

PINCERS: FLUSH CUT (large)
Flush cut pincers are used for tugging out nails and headless tacks from the frame. Choose the size best suited to the task.

MALLET
A mallet is used to drive the ripping chisel

LONG-NOSE PLIERS
Long-nose pliers have a useful tweezer action for tacks and staples that are difficult to reach.

BERRY-TYPE STAPLE REMOVER
Some people tend to over-staple without considering the problems this may cause for the next upholsterer. Staple removers are a useful piece of equipment.

STRAIGHT-HANDLED RIPPING CHISEL
Use it with the mallet to lift out old tacks.

STAPLE REMOVER
The forked shape makes it easy to remove deeply embedded tacks, staples or studs.

TOOLS FOR REBUILDING

There are many different upholstery tools. The selection shown here will allow you to achieve all the projects in this book.

MAGNETIC HAMMER

A two-ended hammer with one end magnetized is an essential tool. It allows you to pick up tacks with one hand, leaving your other hand free to hold material taut. Pick up and knock in the tacks with the magnetic end, then turn the hammer around and drive the tack home.

SLOT-AND-PEG WEBBING STRETCHER (above left)

Another essential tool, this is the only way to get webbing stretched tight enough.

GOOSE-NECKED WEBBING STRETCHER (above right)

Not essential if you have the slot-and-peg type of stretcher but, with its padded head, this type is useful for webbing onto a curved frame and to protect show-wood. Goose-necked webbing stretchers are more commonly used throughout North America.

A SELECTION OF SHEARS

The shears in the middle are the basic tool. The short-bladed pair on the left are useful for cutting through tough layers of fabric. The shears on the right are for left-handed people.

TAILOR'S CHALK

While the work is in progress, use tailor's chalk to mark center points or stitching distances and then to mark out the top cover. Buy tailor's chalk in a selection of colors to match your top covers, as it does not easily brush off.

WOODEN PLEATING TOOL
This is useful for tucking and folding neat corners.

CURVED NEEDLES
Above: 8-, 6- and 3-in. needles. The larger needles are used for bridle ties and stuffing ties; the smaller ones are for stitching top covers and muslin.

REGULATOR
A regulator is used to distribute stuffing evenly. The broad end may be used to neaten pleating.

DOUBLE-ENDED STRAIGHT NEEDLES
Thse are essential for buttoning, blind- and topstitching and making stuffing ties.

YARDSTICK
Use this as a straight edge to draw around and cut out the top cover.

FABRIC TAPE
A fabric tape measure is easy to hang around your neck while working and to use to measure around seat pads.

UPHOLSTERER'S LOOP PINS
These are longer and stronger than pins, and are used to anchor fabric in position.

RETRACTABLE METAL TAPE
Use for measuring out large pieces of fabric.

SLIDING BEVEL
This is used to measure the height of stuffing at the edge of the pad.

MATERIALS

The materials shown here are traditional, but also fit today's demands for sustainable and natural products.

TACKS

From left to right: ⅝-in. (16-mm); ½-in. (13-mm); ⅜-in. (10-mm) improved; ¼-in. (6-mm). In traditional upholstery, tacks are used to secure each stage of the work and you will need a selection of sizes. "Improved" tacks have a large head on a stout shank and are used for securing webbing, burlap, and temporary tacking. "Fine" tacks are used for securing linen scrim, muslin, wadding and the top cover.

GIMP PINS

Available in a selection of colors, these tiny painted pins are used to fasten trimmings unobtrusively.

ITALIAN HEMP TWINE

This tough hemp twine is sturdy enough to tie down the springs.

3-PLY JUTE CORD

This is used for most of the stitching work while building the pad: for making stuffing ties and bridle ties, topstitching and blind stitching. A helpful tip to stop your cord from becoming entangled is to put it into a small bag, as shown on the left.

REEL AND SKEIN OF WAXED SLIPPING THREAD

Available in various colors, slipping thread is used for slipstitching the top cover and for sewing on trims.

BLACK-AND-WHITE WEBBING

This herringbone webbing is the strongest webbing available and should always be used on seats as it provides the platform for the rest of the work.

10-LB JUTE WEBBING

This can be used on backs and arms.

HORSETAIL HAIR

This is the queen of stuffings. Curled horsehair is springy and less likely to poke through the muslin than cheaper stuffings. It's expensive, of course. Save yourself money by retrieving old horsehair when you are stripping. Wash it and tease out clumps.

MIXED ANIMAL HAIR

Likely to include short hairs but cheaper than horsehair.

BLACK POLISHED FIBER

Cheaper still, this is dyed, fire-retardant coconut hair.

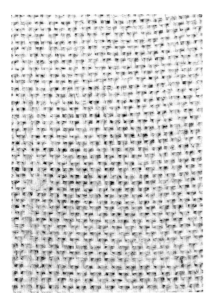

10-OZ BURLAP
This is the heaviest and strongest burlap and covers webbing and springs. Made from jute, it is tough yet flexible and gives long service.

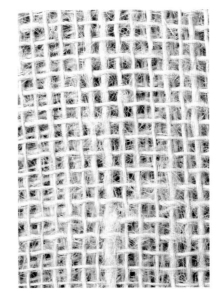

7-OZ BURLAP
With a looser weave, 7-oz burlap is flexible and can be used as a cheaper standin for scrim for covering stuffing and for other non-loadbearing roles.

LINEN SCRIM
The loose, open weave of scrim makes it flexible enough to hold stitches and ties and gives a sturdy edge.

MUSLIN
This strong, unbleached cotton provides the undergarment for the top cover, taking all the tension so that the top cover takes as little strain as possible. It can also be used for lining and as bottom cloth.

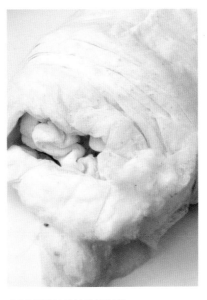

COTTON WADDING
Cotton wadding has a tissue paper back, which holds the fibers in place. It is supplied folded in half, with the fibers innermost. It is a thin wadding that is placed on top of the muslin, paper side up, before the top cover is set on. This protects the top cover from escaping prickles of stuffing.

COTTON FELT
Also known as linter felt, this wadding has a brown paper backing to hold it together, which is removed when used. It can be used to bulk out cotton wadding, as a thin wadding on its own, or as a final stuffing.

Knots, stitches, and trims

Master these knots, stitches, and trimming techniques and all the projects in this book will be within your grasp.

We have selected a few simple and effective knots and stitches. Several are simply versions of others used for different steps. Locking-back stitch, blind stitch, and topstitch, for example, all work on the basic backstitch principle.

As you work through the book, you will use the same techniques again and again, and will find they become second nature to you. If you get stuck, refer back to the clear step-by-step instructions that follow.

We have also included instructions on piping to extend your creative range.

KNOTS

CLOVE HITCH KNOT

Clove hitch knots are used to attach Italian hemp twine to springs.

1 Pass the twine over the coil and bring the uattached length up and around.

2 Bring the twine back toward you, holding the knot tight with your finger.

3 Cross the shorter end over the attached twine, and pass the end up between them.

4 Pull the shorter length toward you to tighten the knot.

DOUBLE SLIP KNOT
Slip knots are used to fasten on twine or cord securely.

1 Thread a curved needle with cord, insert the needle into the fabric from the front and bring back up again about ½ in. (1.25 cm) further along. Pull the needle through, leaving a tail of cord about 3 in. (7.5 cm) long.

2 Hold both ends of the cord in one hand to form a loop and take the short free end in your working hand.

3 Pass the shorter piece of cord over the two strands, then bring it up through the loop.

4 Repeat the action.

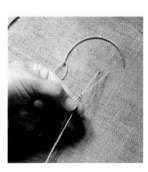

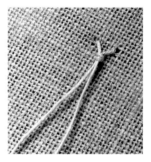

5 Pull tight, then slide the knot upward, pulling on the longer length of cord.

6 Double slip knot.

HALF-HITCH KNOT
The half-hitch knot is used to sew the base of the spring to the webbing. It's used again when you tack the burlap over the springs to secure the top of the spring to the burlap. The half-hitch knot is also useful for fastening off. Make two or three.

1 Use a curved needle and 3-ply jute cord. Stitch over the spring, as shown, then, onthe underside, slip your needle through the loop to knot it. Reverse the procedure to stitch to the burlap.

2 The underside of the webbing will look like this.

3 The stitches at the base of the spring look like this.

STITCHES

STUFFING TIES

Stuffing ties are long, looped stitches that hold stuffing in place. Use 3-ply jute cord and a 5-in. 15-gauge needle.

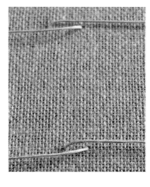

1 Draw a chalk cross marking the center of the burlap as a guide for the stuffing ties. Aim for a sort of right angle zigzag, similar to that shown above.

2 Start by making a slip knot in the back lefthand corner. Backstitch under your center line, so you have two long stitches across the width of your seat.

3 Make a stitch down the side and, backstitching again, turn to make two more stitches crosswise. Continue until you reach the front.

4 The stitches should be just tight enough for you to be able to put two fingers through. Make sure you don't take up the slack as you work. If you're satisfied, tie off the cord.

BRIDLE TIES

Bridle ties are long, deep stitches that hold the pad to the base burlap.

1 Thread a long, double-ended needle with 3-ply jute cord. If it makes it easier, draw out your quartered square with tailor's chalk. Starting in the back lefthand corner, stick your needle through the pad. Keeping it upright, bring it back up close by your first point of entry and make a slip knot.

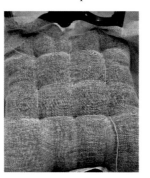

2 Make long backstitches, bringing the needle back up through the pad slightly before the point at which it entered. Your stitches need to be firmly pulled through to create a dimpling effect on the pad. Tie off each bridle tie with a half-hitch to support the filling as you work. Fasten off.

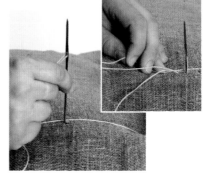

BLIND STITCH

Blind stitching is the first step toward turning the rounded sides of your pad into square, upright sides. First, regulate well.

1 Using your yardstick and tailor's chalk, mark along the sides of the pad at intervals of about 1 in. (2.5 cm).

2 Cut a long length of 3-ply jute cord, thread your double-ended, straight needle, and make a slip knot at the vertical side of the left upright.

3 Working from your second chalk mark, insert the unthreaded end of the needle just above the tack line at an angle, so that it emerges on the outside of the bridle ties.

4 Tilt the needle slightly so that it loops over the stuffing and push it back through so that it comes out at your first chalk mark. Again, don't pull it all the way through—3 in. (7.5 cm) will suffice.

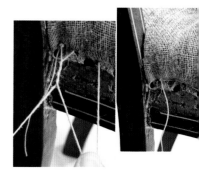

5 Pull the needle through until the threaded eye is just showing (don't pull it all the way out).

6 Wind the cord three times around the needle.

7 Holding the cord, pull the needle all the way out.

8 Pull the stitch tight. Insert the needle at the next chalk mark, returning to the end of your previous stitch.

TOPSTITCH

Topstitching gives a sturdy, square top edge to your pad. Regulate (see page 43) before you start stitching to make sure that there will be sufficient stuffing to make a firm top-stitch roll.

1 Chalk a straight line on the top of your pad 1 in. (2.5 cm) from the edge. Using the same chalk marks on the side as a guide, start work 1 in. (2.5 cm) below the top. Use the same backstitch principle as for blind stitching but this time draw the needle all the way through. Make your stitches about 1 in. (2.5 cm) long.

2 Again, work back to the previous stitch.

3 Wind the twine around the needle three times.

4 Pull the stitch taut.

5 Keep regulating as you work, bringing stuffing forward into the roll.

SLIPSTITCH

This is an essential stitch for invisible seams. It is sometimes called Castle stitch because of the castellated effect of stitching on alternate sides. Slipstitch can also be used to join two pieces of fabric; see the box cushion (page 120).

1 Using a small curved needle and waxed slipping thread, make a knot in your thread and hide it behind the piping. Make your first stitch on the seat pad, behind the piping where the thread emerged.

2 Make your next stitch in the piping, again just behind the point at which the thread emerges and well hidden at the back. Pull the stitches tight as you work.

BLANKET STITCH

Blanket stitch is a sturdy joining stitch and can be used to sew up corners in the unseen layers. In the Edwardian recliner project (see page 110), it is used to secure the burlap to the top of the spring unit.

1 Using 3-ply jute cord and a curved needle, make a slip knot to start. Stick the needle through the fabric without pulling the twine tight.

2 Pull the needle out and back through the loop of cord. Pull tight.

LOCKING-BACK STITCH

Locking-back stitch is used to secure a pad to the base hessian, particularly on the backs of chairs: see the gilded chair (page 86). It is also used to secure piping: see the long footstool (page 58).

Using a 5-in 15-gauge curved needle and 3-ply jute cord, make a backstitch about 1 in. (2.5 cm) long, winding the thread three times around the needle before pulling the thread through.

TRIMS

PIPING

When you want to maintain the integrity of your fabric and feel that braid would be an unnecessary distraction, piping is the answer. With some fabrics it makes sense to cut your fabric on the bias. This gives it extra flexibility and you can get longer lengths. It may also be a design decision. If you are using a checked fabric, this will give you a diagonal contrast. If you plan to make the piping to match the top cover, do remember that you will need to order more fabric.

To make piping you need to fit a piping foot onto your sewing machine. These are found in most haberdasheries. Our

picture shows three types. From the left: double-piping foot, a single-piping foot and a standard sewing machine foot.

SINGLE PIPING

Single piping is made by folding a length of fabric over a single length of piping cord and stitching close to the cord. It has a raw edge to which the top cover is slipstitched or machine sewn. See the Edwardian recliner (page 110), the long footstool (page 58) and the day bed (page 124).

1 Fit a single-piping foot to your sewing machine. Cut a length of fabric about 1½ in. (4 cm) wide to fold over the piping cord.

2 Fold the fabric strip in half, enclosing the piping cord, and machine stitch close to the cord. Trim the raw edges to leave ¼ in. (0.5 cm) beyond the stitching line.

DOUBLE PIPING

Double piping has no raw edges and is glued into place as a trim.

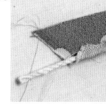

1 Measure how much piping you need. Using tailor's chalk, mark a strip of fabric to this length and 2 in. (5 cm) wide.

2 Pin and machine stitch several pieces together to achieve the required length if necessary.

3 Stitch the seam with the ordinary sewing machine foot. Trim the edges and press the seam on the right side.

4 Fit the double-piping foot. Fold the edge of the fabric over the cord and sew.

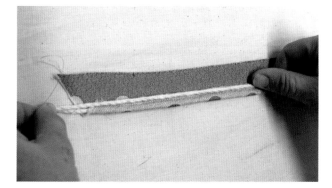 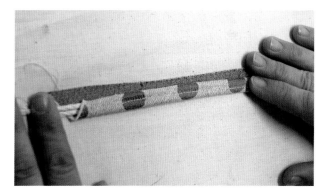

5 Lay another length of piping next to it.

6 Fold the fabric over as shown.

  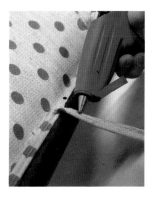

7 Stitch over the seam again; it will now lie between the two lengths of piping cord.

8 Trim off surplus fabric, ensuring that the raw edge is concealed under the piping.

9 The double piping is now ready to be glued in place.

Choosing the fabric and trimmings

You've tucked and tacked, perfected top rolls and scrolls, blind stitched and slipstitched; choosing fabrics and trims is the time to let your imagination, inspiration and creativity loose.

Choose the trimming with the fabric. You can play it safe with a matching braid that covers the tack line or use a trim as a stunning feature. Your choice of fabric will evoke a mood and a style, and each project offers many possibilities.

THE SEXY
The headboard was a sexy piece, reminding us of the Dali sofa shaped as Mae West's lips. The intense, vibrant pink is a stunning statement in a bedroom.

THE AIRY
Roses and parrots and soft white paint transformed this day bed into a delicate and exceptionally pretty piece of furniture.

THE PRACTICALITIES

Let your imagination run away with you, but allow your still small voice of calm to remind you of practicalities.

• Hold the fabric in your hand before you make the decision to buy. Don't rely on pictures from the Internet or magazines. A 4-in. (10-cm) square sample is useful, but most companies will lend you a larger piece of fabric, big enough to drape and give a true impression of weight, texture, and size of pattern.

• Not all fabrics are suitable for all purposes. One that may be fine for curtains will not suit a much-used armchair. Also consider fire-retardant fabrics. Be guided by the fabric companies.

• Don't forget pattern repeats. For a large pattern, such as the parrots and roses on the day bed, more fabric is needed for pattern matching. Be guided by your supplier.

• Take into account your lifestyle. If you have four children and a dog, white may not be the most sensible choice for your sitting room. If you do your upholstery groundwork well, you can always recover later.

• If you are buttoning the back of a chair, remember that the pleating will distort a large patterned fabric. A small repeating pattern or plain fabric may be the best choice.

• Rules are made to be broken but consider carefully first.

THE SPLENDID

Square, unornamented grandeur may be your style. This footstool with its slender legs could have been a delicate piece. Instead, we chose a very strong striped fabric in a combination of colors that was very contemporary. There is nothing of the stuffy smoking room about the lime green, chocolate and violet.

THE PICTORIAL

One of the joys of upholstering small chairs is that you can pick out your favorite section of a pictorial fabric and give it prominence. This simple little wooden chair acted as a frame for a vase of flowers, a section from a delicately colored, watercolor-effect printed linen.

THE WHIMSICAL

The interest in this piece was its roundness. We shot off at a tangent and chose a plaid, the pattern full of squares. The effect was transforming, both to the fabric and the stool. The straight lines of the plaid became arcs and the stool gained a very masculine solidity.

THE ECHOES

In your fabric and trim, echo features of the frame or the fabric itself. We took a section of fabric that echoed the shape of the splat (the molded panel in the middle of the back). Unconventionally, we didn't center the pattern but set the point of interest at the small flower in the center of the back, which leads the eye up the back of the chair. Then, in case anyone had missed the point, we added a trim of pompoms which echoed the seed pod motif in the middle of the chair.

THE TRADITIONAL WITH A TWIST

We wanted to preserve the Victorian elegance of this beautiful rosewood chair. A large pattern would have dwarfed the very fine details of the lovely carving, yet we balked at the ordinariness of a plain or traditional sprigged pattern. We chose dots; we were still using a small, repeating pattern but the simplicity of the dots gives a fresh and modern twist without compromising the character of the chair.

THE RECYCLED

The ethos behind this book is that recycling and sustainability is the truly modern way. Find fabric for your projects that started life as something quite different. Sweetly embroidered in faded red in one corner, this vintage French linen sheet had seen better days. We managed to cut out the unworn parts and made a charming box cushion for an 18th-century pew.

THE
PROJECTS

With your essential tools and materials to hand, you are now ready to start the projects. As you would a recipe, read through your chosen project before you begin. Check that you have the necessary tools and materials, which you will find listed at the opening of each project. Read through the Order of Work, which is a clear list of the steps you need to follow. Simple cross references enable you to refer back to earlier projects as you work, to remind yourself of techniques that have already been covered.

Dining chair drop-in seat

This was an old set of inexpensive, dingy brown, 1940s dining chairs, which we painted with a soft white paint and combined with the classic prettiness of a black-and-white toile de Jouy to create a fresh, modern look.

A drop-in seat for a dining chair is formed by making a stuffed pad on a wooden seat frame and is the ideal first project for a beginner. As you master the techniques, following the simple step-by-step instructions, you will be learning basic principles that you will use in all the projects in this book.

TOOLS

Ripping chisel or staple remover
Mallet
G-clamp
Magnetic hammer
Webbing stretcher
Tailor's shears
Tape measure
Tailor's chalk
5-in. 15-gauge curved needle
Yardstick

MATERIALS

Tacks: ½-in. improved, ⅜-in. improved, ⅜-in. fine
3-ply jute cord
Black-and-white webbing
10-oz burlap
Horsehair
Muslin
Cotton wadding
Top cover
Bottom cloth

ORDER OF WORK

1 Strip (see page 26).

2 Position and fix the webbing (see page 26.

3 Fix the burlap base (see page 28).

4 Make the stuffing ties (see page 30).

5 Stuff with horsehair (see page 31).

6 Measure, cut out and set on the muslin (see page 32).

7 Lay on cotton wadding (see page 32).

8 Measure, cut out and set on the top cover (see page 33).

9 Neaten the top-cover corners (see page 34).

10 Finish with the bottom cloth (see page 35).

THE ORIGINAL CHAIR
Discovered in a junk shop, these chairs were covered in a scuffed, unattractive, brown varnish and had definitely seen better days.

STRIPPING

Prepare for stripping by laying out a protective cloth on your work surface to catch the debris that may come away with the old upholstery. Placing a folded blanket underneath will give a thick, protective layer. Remove the seat from the chair by pushing it up from underneath. It's important not to simply cover the pad with a new piece of material, as this will enlarge the pad and splay the joints of the chair. As you take the pad apart, make a note of the formation of the existing upholstery. You can then copy the webbing pattern when you rebuild the seat.

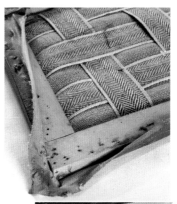

1 Using a G-clamp to hold the seat firmly, take a ripping chisel and mallet and, following the grain of the wood to avoid splitting, knock out the tacks and lift away the layers of old materials and webbing. Keep a vacuum cleaner to hand to clear up mess and stray tacks as you work. It is advisable to wear a paper dust mask.

Right: The upholstery materials and techniques used in the original pad can give you clues to the item's provenance.

FIXING THE WEBBING

The webbing provides a firm base for the pad and should be interwoven and evenly spaced. Here, the original webbing pattern has been copied.

2(a) Clamp the seat firmly to your work surface. Mark the center of each rail with chalk. Using a yardstick, draw a line ¾ in. (2 cm) in from the edge of the rail. Fold under the end of the webbing (do not cut it from the roll). Place the folded end inside the chalked line.

2(b) Using ½-in. improved tacks and a magnetic hammer, hammer three tacks halfway in (so they can be removed if necessary; this is known as "temporary tacking") near the fold, spacing evenly. *Inset:* Temporary tack two tacks beneath to form a W-shape (less likely to split the wood), then knock all tacks firmly in.

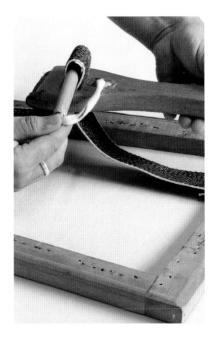

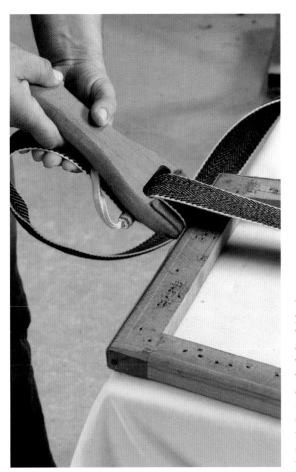

2(c) Hold the handle of the webbing stretcher away from you, with the tie and the post above. Insert the webbing into the stretcher, pulling it through from underneath to form a loop, then place the post in the loop and pull tight.

2(d) Bring the handle of the stretcher over toward you, holding the excess webbing firmly against it, and adjust until the webbing is taut. Pluck the webbing as though it were a guitar string: when it resonates, the tension is correct. Do not over tighten the webbing, as the strain could break the joints of the frame.

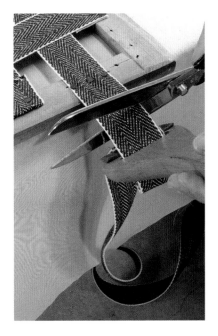

2(e) Holding the webbing stretcher taut with your knee or hip, knock in a row of three tacks close to the inside edge of the chalk line. Cut the webbing, leaving 2 in. (5 cm) overhanging the chalk line.

2(f) Continue in the same way, interweaving the webs.

2(g) Fold the webbing ends over. Knock in two tacks so that you are repeating the W-shape from Step 2(b) (although only the bottom two tacks will be visible).

FIXING THE BURLAP BASE

Burlap provides a strong platform on which to build the pad. Use 10-oz. burlap for its heavy, closely woven strength. It is good practice to start with a square edge, to keep the roll of burlap in good order.

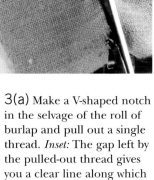

3(a) Make a V-shaped notch in the selvage of the roll of burlap and pull out a single thread. *Inset:* The gap left by the pulled-out thread gives you a clear line along which to cut.

3(b) Lay the webbed frame on the burlap, with a straight edge alongside, butting up to the edge of the frame.

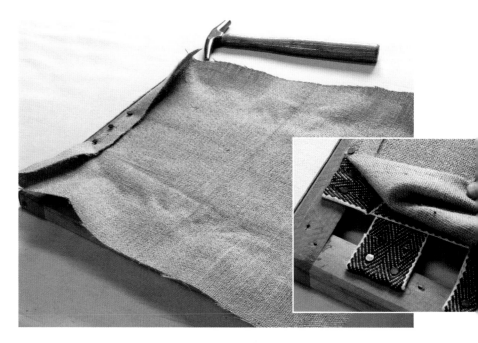

3(c) Using tailor's chalk, draw a line along the edge of the straight edge. This will give you a 1-in. (2.5-cm) overlap. Cut out.

3(d) Set on the burlap, keeping it square. Starting on the back rail, fold the edge of burlap over and temporary tack in the center, using three ⅜ in. improved tacks. Avoid tacking through the webs.

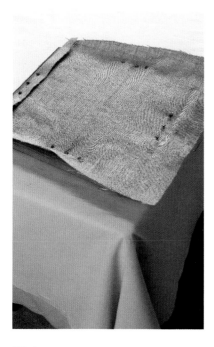

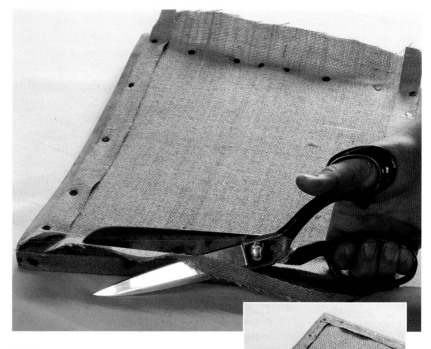

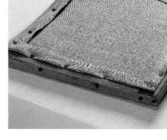

3(e) Without folding the burlap, pull it tight and temporary tack three tacks in the center of the front rail. Do the same on the sides, without folding over the overlap. When you're happy with the positioning, drive all the tacks home.

3(f) Continue tacking, working out from the center. Tack each side of the webbing and in the corners, inserting a tack every 2 in. (5 cm) or so. (Use your judgement: we added an extra tack between the webs.) Trim the edges and tack down the overlap, starting at the corners to maintain tension, then adding another three or four tacks to hold it down.

MAKING THE STUFFING TIES

Stuffiing ties are loosely sewn loops of cord that hold the horsehair in position.

4(a) Draw a chalk cross marking the center of the burlap as a guide for where to place the stuffing ties. Thread a 5-in. 15-gauge curved needle with 3-ply jute cord. Make a slip knot (see page 15) in the back lefthand corner. Backstitch under the center line, and then again at the back righthand corner, so that you have two long stitches across the width of the seat. Make a stitch down the side and, backstitching again, turn to make two more stitches crosswise. *Inset*: Continue until you reach the front of the frame.

4(b) Check the tightness of the stitches. They should be just tight enough for you to be able to put four fingers under each stitch. Once you are satisfied, tie off the cord with a half-hitch knot (see page 15).

4(c) Aim for a similar pattern of ties to the one shown here.

STUFFING WITH HORSEHAIR

Horsehair provides springiness, comfort and bulk for your seat pad.

5(b) Using an upholstery loop pin, check that the horsehair is an even depth across the seat. Aim for a depth of around 1¼ in. (3 cm).

5(a) Teasing out any lumps in the horsehair, push it under the stuffing ties, being careful not to form heavy clumps, until the seat is covered.

5(c) Keeping your hands flat, press down on the horsehair to find any lumps or unevenness. Adjust accordingly.

5(d) Tousle the horsehair gently with your fingertips to fluff it up and knit the fibers of the horsehair together.

5(e) Now work on the edges, building them up with more hair if necessary, pushing it in from underneath and rolling slightly to keep the stuffing to the edge of the wood. If you let it come over the sides, it will make the pad too thick and you'll risk popping the joints of the chair frame when you drop in the seat.

SETTING ON THE MUSLIN

The muslin provides the underdressing and is useful practice for cutting out and fitting the top cover.

6(a) Turn the pad upside down and measure to the inside of the frame each side at the widest part, and then the same from back to front. Cut out the muslin to these measurements.

6(b) Lay the frame on the muslin, horsehair side down. Pulling the muslin square and taut, hammer temporary tacks in the center of each side on the underside of the rail. Ease the fabric diagonally, tacking corners alternately. This holds the muslin in position for the next step.

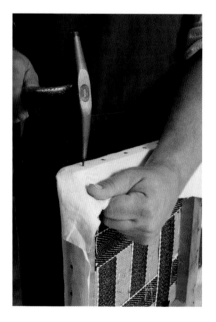

6(c) Stand the pad on its side and, using ⅜ in. fine tacks and working out from the center, and from one opposite side to the other as you did with the burlap, tack the muslin to the side of the frame. Make sure that the tacks are driven in, with no heads standing proud. As you work, smooth the muslin from the bottom with your hand to keep it taut, and tuck up any stray strands of horsehair. Stop 2 in. (5 cm) short of the corners to give room to tuck the corners in.

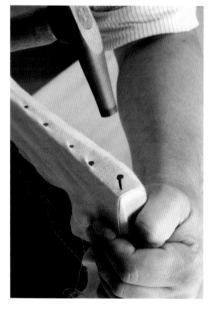

6(d) You can now remove the temporary tacks on the underside. Fold the corners neatly and tack down. Trim the muslin level with the bottom of the frame.

LAYING ON THE COTTON WADDING

Cotton wadding stops any prickliness from the horsehair. It comes folded in two, with the furry side inside and paper on the outside.

7 Open out the cotton wadding and, drawing around your pad, cut it to size. It should just creep over the edge and not add any bulk to the sides of your pad. Lay it on the muslin, furry side down. Add another layer of cotton wadding if you can still feel the prickliness of the horsehair.

SETTING ON THE TOP COVER

If you have fitted the muslin well, it will hold the pad in shape.
Then you just need to lay on the top cover.

8(a) Spread out the fabric and decide which part of the pattern you want to use to cover the chairs. The repeating pattern of this toile de Jouy means that there will be some waste of cloth.

8(b) Refer back to the steps for measuring the muslin. Measure the width of your seat at the widest point, taking the tape to the inside of the rail on both sides. Likewise, measure the length. This will give you a margin of error. Mark lightly on your fabric where you want the center of the seat, using tailor's chalk as close to the background color as possible. Here we used white. Do not use pencil, as you will not be able to erase it if you make a mistake. From the center, mark out your measurements using the yardstick and chalk. Recheck your measurements (a false cut could be an expensive mistake at this point). When you're satisfied you've got it right, cut out the fabric. Lay the panel over the pad to check the fit and pattern. When you're satisfied, cut out the panels for all the chairs in the set.

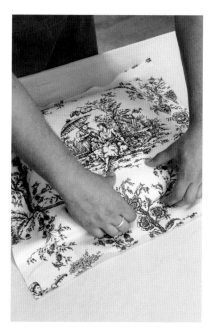

8(c) Smooth the fabric over the pad so that it is square and centered. If you are making a matching set of dining chairs, always refer back to the first to check that the positioning is the same.

8(d) Using ⅜-in. fine tacks, temporary tack three tacks in the center of the first rail, just as you did with the muslin, smoothing the fabric with your hand as you work to keep it centered and taut. Then tack the opposite rail, to insure that your centered fabric doesn't slip out of position, and the two remaining sides. When satisfied, tack to within 1 in. (2.5 cm) of the corners. Tack down the corner flaps, with the point to the middle.

MAKING NEAT CORNERS

Approach snipping into the corners with caution. Read through and make sure you have understood the instructions. If you are unsure, practice on a scrap of muslin.

9(b) Tuck in the corners as shown, making a neat fold and keeping the fabric on the side of the rail smooth. Tack down.

9(a) This technique should be used on all four corners. Make two cuts toward the corner, just up to the corner tack, giving a kipper-tie shape. Cut this off just below the corner tack, being very careful not to take the cuts too far.

9(c) Turn the seat 90 degrees and repeat with the loose flap of fabric. Although it doesn't matter which flap you fold first, try to be consistent. When all corners are finished, trim off any excess fabric.

SETTING ON THE
BOTTOM CLOTH

This is the final stage of most projects. It hides raw edges and prevents dust from falling through.

10(a) Black bottom cloth can be used but because of the lightness of the fabric in this piece, we chose muslin. As you did with the 10-oz burlap, place the seat pad on the muslin, marking it out slightly larger with chalk and your yardstick, and cut out.

10(b) Set on the muslin, folding under the edges, and tack, using ⅜ in. fine tacks. Use more tacks on the front edge, which gets more wear. Temporary tacking is advisable, until you are sure the muslin is set squarely.

Pin-stuffed chair

This unusual little chair with faux ivory detailing had a cane seat, which had fallen through. As a professional repair would be prohibitively expensive we decided to pin-stuff it, which makes only a thin pad and is probably the simplest way to upholster a chair seat. We then covered it with a highly pictorial gray linen printed with vases of flowers in subtle colors. We used a toning trim around the edge, as a contrasting color would have the effect of diminishing the pad.

In addition to the basic techniques covered in the dining chair with drop-in seat on page 24, this project introduces gluing on a trim, neatening frayed edges, concealing the join, making a neat turn and how to avoid getting glue on your precious and expensive fabric.

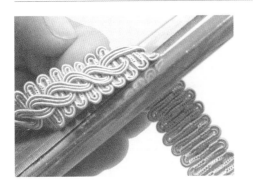

TOOLS

Ripping chisel or staple remover
Mallet
Magnetic hammer
Webbing stretcher
Tailor's shears
Tape measure
Tailor's chalk
5-in. 15-gauge curved needle
Upholsterer's loop pins
Hot glue gun and glue sticks

MATERIALS

Black-and-white webbing
10-oz burlap
Tacks: ½-in. improved, ⅜-in. fine
Horsehair
Muslin
Cotton wadding
Top cover
Braid
Gimp pins, color to match braid

ORDER OF WORK

1 Strip (see page 26).

2 Position and fix the webbing (see page 26).

3 Fix the burlap base (see page 28).

4 Make the stuffing ties (see page 30).

5 Stuff with horsehair (see page 31).

6 Measure, cut out and set on the muslin (see page 32).

7 Lay on cotton wadding (see page 32).

8 Measure, cut out and set on the top cover (see page 33).

9 Attach the trim (see page 38).

THE ORIGINAL CHAIR
Although the original cane seat was in a very sorry state of repair, the framework of the chair was in generally good order. A simple pin-stuffed seat, fixed directly onto the frame, seemed the obvious solution.

POINTS TO WATCH

Up to Stage 8, at which you set on the top cover, the stages are similar to those for the drop-in seat on page 24. Follow the Order of Work on page 37, but take note of the following points:

• Tack everything directly on to the chair frame.

• Set on the burlap, tacking into the existing tack line, and stitch stuffing ties.

• The horsehair should not be overdone. Aim to create a gentle hummock, or "crown," as it is known in the upholstery trade.

FIXING THE WEBBING
Position the webbing on top of the rail, with the edges aligning with the tack marks of the old cane seat. Because this is a small chair, we used only four webs – three from back to front and one from side to side.

BUILDING UP THE LAYERS
As for the drop-in seat, the webbing is followed by burlap, stuffing ties, horsehair, muslin and cotton wadding.

SETTING ON THE TOP COVER
Tuck under the edges of the fabric. Although the tacks will be hidden by braid, you need to achieve a neat edge with the tacks aligned and well driven in.

ATTACHING THE TRIM

Caution and care cannot be overemphasized here. After all your hard work, a misplaced blob of adhesive at this final stage would be heartbreaking. Practice with the glue gun first, so that you can control the flow of adhesive.

9(a) The first step is to neaten the edge of your inevitably fraying braid. Place a small blob of adhesive on the back of the braid about 2 in. (5 cm) from the end.

9(b) Fold the end over at a right angle, as shown, and press hard together.

9(c) With the right side of the braid facing upward, trim off the fraying end, making sure that the cut side is well concealed underneath. This will give a neat diagonal end to your braid.

9(d) Using a loop pin to hold the braid in place, choose a gimp pin to match the color of the braid and temporary tack it at the back righthand corner, with the slant of the diagonal pattern of the braid facing inward.

9(e) Start gluing the back of the braid. Work on 4-in. (10-cm) sections and hold the braid well away from the fabric. Position the braid carefully, following the edge of the top cover to hide the tacks.

9(f) Make a neat fold at the corners and use loop pins to hold the braid in place. Glue carefully, forming a miter rather than a right-angle fold.

9(g) To finish off, make another diagonal fold to join perfectly at the point where the braid began. Hold with a loop pin and secure with a gimp pin.

9(h) Knock in the gimp pins and, if your braid allows it, use a loop pin to reposition strands of the braid to hide the heads of the gimp pins.

Stuff-over pad for inlaid bedroom chair

The delicate detailing of this pretty bedroom chair was marred by the dour, dull-green velvet with which it had been covered. A patterned fabric would have fought with the intricacy of the inlay, so we chose an off-white Ottoman rib, a hard-wearing ribbed cotton, which picks up the light-colored detailing. The pink and cream trim adds a frivolous finishing touch.

This project introduces building up a pad using blind stitching and topstitching. The pad is built up on the frame of the chair itself, rather than on a separate frame as with the drop-in seat on page 24.

TOOLS

Ripping chisel or staple remover
Mallet
Magnetic hammer
Webbing stretcher
Tailor's shears
Tape measure
Tailor's chalk
5-in. 15-gauge curved needle
Regulator
12-in. double-ended straight needle
Sliding bevel
Hot glue gun and glue sticks

MATERIALS

Tacks: ½-in. improved, ⅜-in. fine
3-ply jute cord
Black-and-white webbing
10-oz burlap
Horsehair
Linen scrim
Muslin
Cotton wadding
Top cover
Braid
Bottom cloth

ORDER OF WORK

1 Strip (see page 26).

2 Fix the webbing (see page 26).

3 Fix the burlap base (see page 28).

4 Make the stuffing ties (see page 30).

5 Stuff with horsehair (see page 31).

6 Set on the scrim (see page 42).

7 Stitch the bridle ties (see page 42).

8 Tack off the scrim (see page 43).

9 Regulate the stuffing (see page 43).

10 Form neat corners (see page 44).

11 Blind stitch (see page 44).

12 Topstitch (see page 46).

13 Stuff with a second layer of horsehair (see page 47).

14 Measure, cut out and set on the muslin (see page 48).

15 Lay on the cotton wadding (see page 48).

16 Measure, cut out and set on the top cover (see page 33).

17 Fold the corners of the top cover (see page 48).

18 Attach the trimming (see pages 38 and 51).

19 Finish with the bottom cloth (see page 35).

THE ORIGINAL CHAIR
The delicate inlay needed a lighter fabric to show it off to best advantage.

POINTS TO WATCH

Up to Stage 5, at which the pad is stuffed with horsehair, the technique is much the same as for the drop-in seat on page 24. Follow the Order of Work on page 41, but note the following points:

• The webbing is positioned on top of the rail.

• Stuffing ties should be slightly looser than on the drop-in seat, to allow for a greater depth of horsehair.

• Be guided by the proportions of your chair as to the depth of the horsehair that is required.

• Use the flat of your hands to mold the horsehair and create the beginnings of the square edges.

CHECKING THE DEPTH OF THE HORSEHAIR
Use your hands (above left) or a sliding bevel (above right) to check the depth of the horsehair.

SETTING ON SCRIM

6 Measure the seat from front to back and from side to side at the widest point and cut the scrim to size, allowing 4 in. (10cm) for turning under. Set on squarely with three temporary tacks at the center of each vertical edge just above the show-wood. We used ⅜-in. fine tacks, because of delicacy of the frame.

STITCHING THE BRIDLE TIES

7(a) The bridle ties are long, deep stitches that hold the pad to the base burlap. With this project, you need to aim for the shape shown here. Thread a long double-ended needle with 3-ply jute cord. If it makes it easier, draw out a quartered square with tailor's chalk. Start with a slip knot (see page 15). Stick the needle through the pad. Keeping it upright, bring it back up close by the first point of entry and finish with a half-hitch knot (see page 15).

7(b) Make long backstitches as shown on page 18, bringing the needle back up through the pad slightly before the point at which it entered. Pull the stitches through firmly to create a dimpling effect on the pad. Fasten off with a clove hitch knot (see page 14).

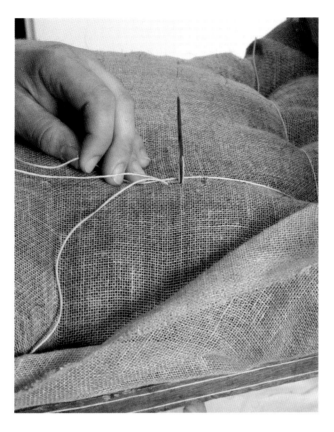

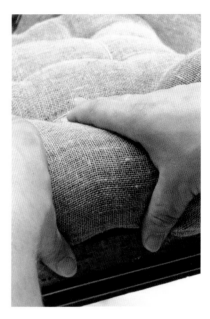

7(c) Remove the temporary tacks one side at a time. At this point, add more horsehair to the edge if needed, treating the edge stuffing as though it were a tube with the bridle ties at the back. Tuck the edges of the scrim under the horsehair.

TACKING OFF SCRIM

REGULATING STUFFING

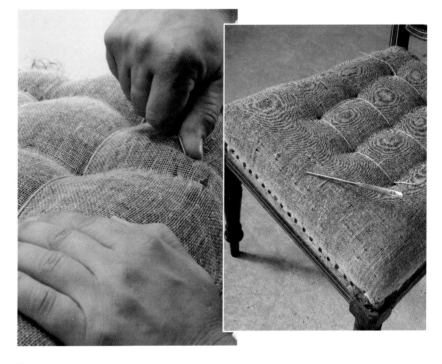

8 Using ⅜-in. fine tacks, tack the scrim's folded edge to the beveled edge of the rail in the middle of each side, leaving the corners untacked. (We used fine, rather than improved, tacks because of the chair's delicate frame.)

9 The regulator is an indispensable tool that allows you to move the stuffing around under the scrim without having to undo tacking. Using your thumb as a depth gauge and pivot, push the pointed end of the regulator into the pad and maneuver it around to even out any inconsistencies in the filling and give a firm, rounded edge.

FORMING NEAT CORNERS

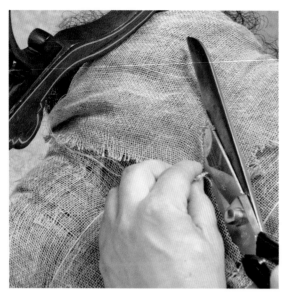

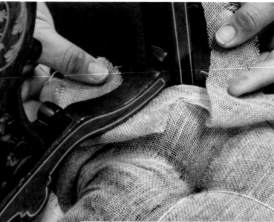

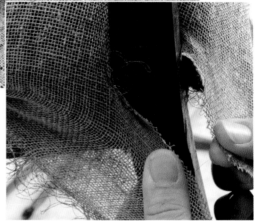

10(a) Now you must deal with the corners. This is good practice for setting on your top cover, when a snip too far would be a serious mistake. Starting at the back, fold back the untacked corner of the scrim and cut from the corner, ½ in. (1.25 cm) short of the edge of the upright.

10(b) Tuck the scrim into the corner, around the upright, pulling on both sides evenly.

BLIND STITCHING

Blind stitching is the first step toward turning the rounded sides of your pad into square, upright sides.

11(a) Using a yardstick and tailor's chalk, mark the sides of the pad at intervals of 1 in. (2.5 cm). This will keep the stitches even, pulling the same amount of stuffing to the edge each time and avoiding getting lumps and bulges in the pad.

11(b) Cut a good length of 3-ply jute cord, thread a 12-in. double-ended straight needle, and make a slip knot at the vertical side of the left upright.

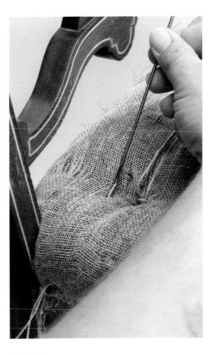

11(c) Working from the second chalk mark, insert the unthreaded end of the needle just above the tack line at an angle so that it emerges on the outside of the bridle ties.

11(d) Pull the needle through until the threaded eye is just showing (do not pull the needle all the way out).

11(e) Tilt the needle slightly so that it loops over the stuffing and push it back through so that it comes out at the first chalk mark. Again, do not pull the needle all the way through—3 in. (7.5 cm) will suffice.

11(f) Wind the cord three times around the needle.

11(g) Holding the cord, pull the needle all the way out.

11(h) Holding the loop with one hand and the cord with the other, pull the stitch tight. Insert the needle at the next chalk mark, returning to the end of the previous stitch.

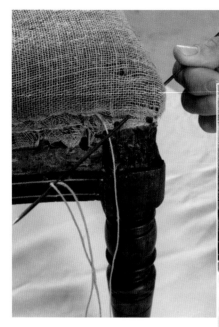

11(i) To create a sharp corner, regulate the stuffing into the corner and slide the needle through diagonally, cutting off the corner. Pull the cord tight and continue blind stitching.

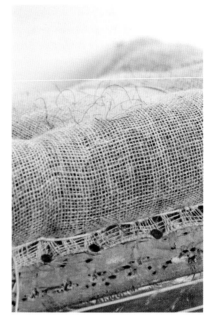

11(j) Continue in this manner until you have stitched around the whole pad. Then, depending on the height of the pad, work a second row of blind stitching about 1 in. (2.5 cm) above the first, following the same chalk marks.

TOPSTITCHING

Topstitching gives a sturdy, square top edge to the pad. Regulate before you start stitching to make sure there is sufficient stuffing for a firm top-stitch roll.

12(a) Chalk a straight line on the top of the pad 1 in. (2.5 cm) from the edge. Using the same chalk marks on the side as a guide, start work 1 in. (2.5 cm) below the top. Use the same backstitch principle as for blind stitching, but this time draw the needle all the way through.

12(b) Again work back toward the previous chalk mark so that the new stitch sits next to the previous stitch.

12(c) Wind the cord around the needle three times.

12(d) Pull the stitch taut.

12(e) Keep regulating as you work, bringing stuffing forward into the roll.

12(f) Continue until all four sides have been stitched.

SECOND LAYER OF HORSEHAIR

Make the stuffing ties and stuff with horsehair in the same way as for the drop-in seat on page 24.

13(b) Make a shallow stuffing of horsehair.

13(a) Stitch the stuffing ties 1½ in. (4 cm) in from the topstitching on all sides and then down the middle from back to front, to hold the second stuffing close to the edge.

MUSLIN AND COTTON WADDING

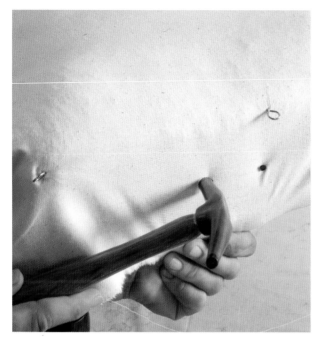

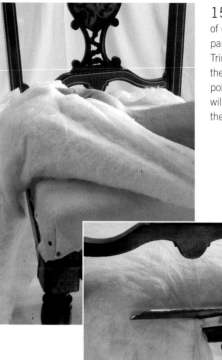

15 Use two layers of cotton wadding, paper side up. Inset: Trim to just above the show-wood—the polished wood that will be visible when the chair is finished.

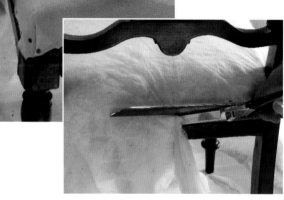

14 Cut the muslin to size. Set on and secure with loop pins while you tack onto the vertical edge, being careful not to tack into the show-wood. Tack down to the tack line, folding the front corners neatly. For the back corners, cut the muslin to the rail. Trim.

TOP COVER

16 The pad is now all but finished. The muslin is taking the strain. Your chosen fabric just needs to lie on it and to fit perfectly. Refer to the instructions on page 33, taking note of the following points:

• Measure the fabric, adding 2 in. (5 cm) to both the length and the width. This will give you 1-in. (2.5-cm) overlap all the way around.

• Mark out with matching chalk. We used a plain, cream Ottoman rib, so centering the pattern is not a problem. If you have chosen a patterned fabric, refer to the guidelines on page 33 for the drop-in seat for the dining chair.

• Temporary tack three tacks in the center of each side. When you are happy with the setting on, tack with ⅜-in. fine, stopping 2 in. (5 cm) short of each corner.

TOP-COVER BACK CORNERS

Corners can be nerve-wracking for the novice, so stay calm and read through the steps before you snip.

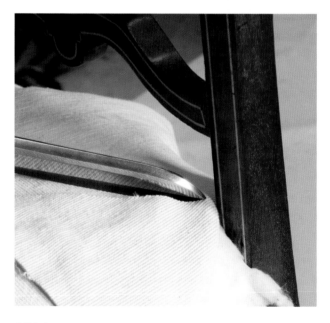

17(a) Starting at the back righthand upright, fold the corner of the fabric back so that the fold snugly touches the upright. Position the shears so that they lie from the corner of the folded-back fabric with the point ½ in. (1.25 cm) from the upright. Cut along that line.

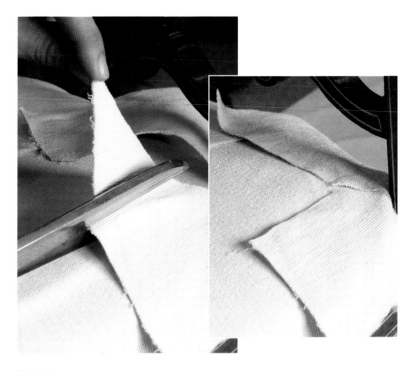

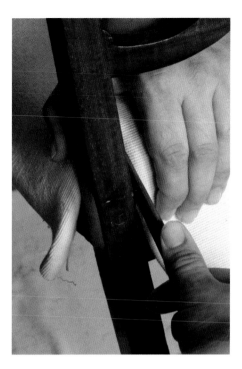

17(b) Trim the flaps, as shown above.

17(c) Fold the raw edges under so that the edges lie flush with the upright, and tack in place, using ⅜-in. fine tacks.

FRONT CORNERS

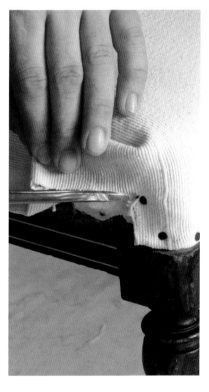

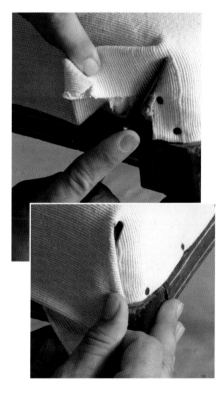

17(d) Smooth the fabric from the front around the corner and tack in place.

17(e) Make a cut, as shown above.

17(f) Fold the fabric over so that the corner is straight and not puckered. Use a wooden pleating tool or the flat end of a regulator to get a sharp fold.

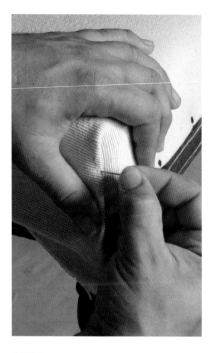

17(h) Using a regulator to hold the fabric in position, tack the corner in place. Remove the pin.

17(g) Remove the pleating tool and pin the fabric in place.

A NEAT FINISH

This back shot of the finished chair shows the neat finish you need to achieve around the back uprights. The fabric is pulled down snugly to the upright with all raw edges tucked in and any wrinkles smoothed out.

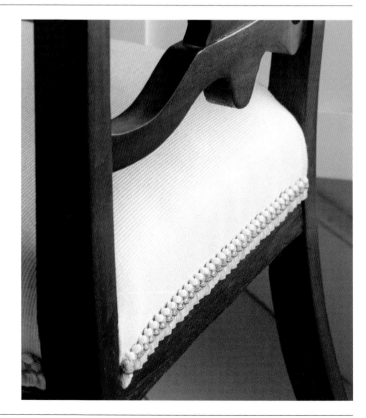

TRIMMING

Trim as described for the pin-stuffed chair, noting that as you are working on the vertical edge, you do not have to negotiate complicated corners.

18(a) Apply glue to neaten frayed ends (see page 38). Cut off the excess.

18(b) Apply glue to short lengths of the trim at a time, keeping the gun away from your top cover.

18(c) You will need a separate short length of trim for the back.

18(d) Tuck under the ends of the braid and glue in place, using gimp pins if necessary.

19 Finish with the bottom cloth.

Victorian piano stool

It was a crime to cover this ornate, Victorian, screw-lift piano stool with such an overstated floral fabric. The stool was in desperate need of loving attention and we chose a warm wool plaid to bring out the color of the wood.

This project demonstrates how checked material can be manipulated to pleasing effect on a round stool, creating decorative arcs in the pattern. We show how over-bunched pleating can be avoided and reuse the skills of blind and topstitching that you have already learnt in the stuff-over pad for the bedroom chair on page 40.

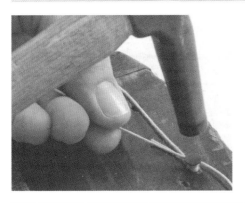

TOOLS

Ripping chisel or staple remover
Mallet
Magnetic hammer
Tailor's shears
Tape measure
Tailor's chalk
5-in. 15-gauge curved needle
Double-ended straight needle
Regulator
Upholsterer's loop pins
Hot glue gun and glue sticks

MATERIALS

Tacks: ½-in. improved, ⅜-in. improved,
   ⅜-in. fine
3-ply jute cord
10-oz burlap
Horsehair
Linen scrim
Muslin
Cotton wadding
Top cover
Braid

ORDER OF WORK

1 Strip (see page 26).

2 Fix the burlap base (see page 54).

3 Make the stuffing ties (see page 54).

4 Stuff with horsehair (see page 55).

5 Set on the scrim (see pages 42 and 55).

6 Stitch the bridle ties (see page 42).

7 Blind stitch (see page 44).

8 Topstitch (see page 46).

9 Stuff a second layer of horsehair (see page 47).

10 Measure, cut out and set on the muslin (see page 56).

11 Lay on the cotton wadding (see page 56).

12 Measure, cut out and set on the top cover (see pages 32 and 56)

13 Attach the trimming (see page 57).

THE ORIGINAL STOOL
The floral pattern of this fabric is too busy and draws attention away from the lovely ornate feet of the stool.

FIXING THE BURLAP BASE AND MAKING THE STUFFING TIES

2 The small square hole in the stool's base requires no webbing. Using ½-in. improved tacks, tack a square of burlap tautly over.

3(a) For the stuffing ties, use ⅜-in. improved tacks and 3-ply jute cord. Knock eight tacks (or more if your project is larger) halfway in, spacing them evenly around the circumference of the stool about 1 in. (2.5 cm) from the edge. Using a slip knot (see page 15), attach the cord.

3(b) Take the cord around the next tack, making sure that you can get four fingers under the stitch. Then knock in the tack to secure. Continue until you arrive back at the first tack.

3(c) Wind the cord around the first tack and knock the tack in firmly.

3(d) Thread the cord into a curved needle and make stuffing ties following the square of the burlap, as shown above. Take the last tie into the middle of the burlap square and tie off.

HORSEHAIR STUFFING

SETTING ON SCRIM

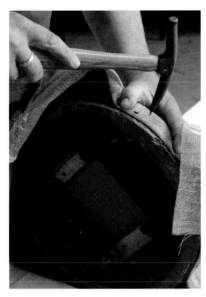

4 Working from the inside of the ties around the circumference of the stool and with a rolling motion to give a high side, tuck the horsehair under the ties. Build up the middle, remembering that you need depth for top- and blind stitching, as with the stuff-over bedroom chair on pages 44–46.

5(a) Cut the scrim to size (see page 42). Using ⅜-in. improved tacks, temporary tack the scrim onto the vertical edge of the stool, folding up the edges of the scrim neatly as you work.

5(b) The scrim must fit tightly enough to hold the horsehair firmly in place.

5(c) Using a double-ended needle, stitch through the center to the burlap and fasten with a slip knot.

BRIDLE TIES, BLIND STITCHING AND TOP-STITCHING, SECOND STUFFING OF HORSEHAIR

6–9 Proceed as for the stuff-over bedroom chair, noting the following points:

- Stitch bridle ties in the form of a square around the slip knot, using your double-ended straight needle to hold the scrim onto the hair and burlap, as for the stuff-over bedroom chair on page 42. When in place, snip out the center slip knot.

- Remember you are working with a circle, not a square.

- Take out temporary tacks as you work, tacking raw edges under onto the beveled edge with ⅜-in. improved tacks.

- Work two rows of blind stitching around the edge and one on top. On a round project keep stitches even, or the pad can become lopsided—try marking with tailor's chalk at 1½-in. (4-cm) intervals around the side.

- Regulate thoroughly before you start stitching—but do not over-regulate or you may find yourself with an accumulated clump of stuffing as you complete the circle.

- As you blind stitch and topstitch, regulate gently from bottom to top, being very careful to keep the pad round not oval.

- Make a thin second stuffing of horsehair.

SETTING ON THE MUSLIN

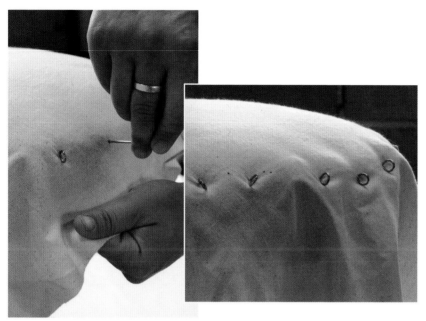

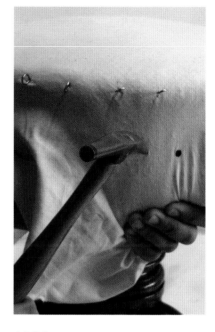

10(a) Cut the muslin to size, set on and secure to the crown of the pad with loop pins, pulling and smoothing the fabric until it is taut. The loop pins take the strain of the top while you tack.

10(b) Tack the muslin to the vertical edge of the stool with ⅜-in. improved tacks. Tack from side to side, pulling on the bias first to lose fullness and minimize pleating.

COTTON WADDING

TOP COVER

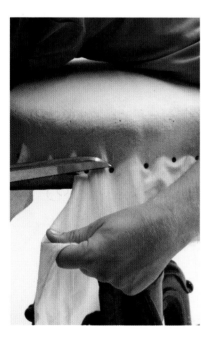

10(c) Trim the muslin close to the tacks and remove the loop pins.

11 Set on the cotton wadding. Measure for the top cover, allowing an extra ¾ in. (2 cm) all around; do not allow too much extra, because you want to keep pleating to a minimum.

12(a) Find a center point (here we used a line in the fabric), then set the top cover on in line with the center of the stool.

12(c) The stretch of this good quality fabric is shown by the arcs in the pattern around the sides of the stool.

13(a) The braid will cover the tacks at the lower edge of the stool. Tack the end of the braid on the wrong side to fix. Keep it in line with the bottom of the stool.

12(b) Temporary tack, turning the stool as you work to keep the stretch of the fabric even. Take out one or two temporary tacks at a time and, turning the raw edges under, tack down in line with the bottom of the frame with ⅜-in. fine tacks. Again, work from one side to the other.

13(b) Fold the braid over the tack so that the right side shows and glue over the tack line, working in small sections at a time. To make the join as neat as possible, fold the end under and glue, so that the start and end of the braid meet exactly. Secure with gimp pins if necessary.

Long footstool

This elegant, slender-legged footstool had obviously been an opulent piece of furniture in its time. We decided to restore it to its former glory by covering it in a beautiful striped velvet fabric in rich purples, greens, and browns, piped around the top and at the bottom.

Although this is a large piece of furniture, the basic principle is the same as for the stuff-over bedroom chair on page 40. Build up the pad with horsehair in exactly the same way, using blind stitching and topstitching, to give strong, straight sides. This project introduces the use of piping.

TOOLS

Ripping chisel or staple remover
Mallet
Magnetic hammer
Webbing stretcher
Tailor's shears
Tape measure and tailor's chalk
5-in. 15-gauge curved needle
Regulator
Double-ended straight needle
Sliding bevel
Sewing machine
Small curved needle
Hot glue gun and glue sticks

MATERIALS

Tacks: ½-in. improved, ⅜-in. improved,
    ⅜-in. fine
3-ply jute cord
Black-and-white webbing
10-oz burlap
Horsehair
Linen scrim
Muslin
Cotton wadding
Top cover
Piping cord
Waxed slipping thread
Bottom cloth

THE ORIGINAL FOOTSTOOL
Covered in a gorgeous, but much worn, yellow brocade, this elegant footstool was in need of tender, loving care.

ORDER OF WORK

1 Strip (see page 26).

2 Position and fix the webbing (see page 26).

3 Fix the burlap base (see page 28).

4 Make the stuffing ties (see page 30).

5 Stuff with horsehair (see page 31).

6 Set on the scrim (see page 42).

7 Stitch the bridle ties (see page 42).

8 Tack off the scrim (see page 43).

9 Regulate the stuffing (see page 43).

10 Blind stitch (see page 44).

11 Topstitch (see page 46).

12 Stuff with a second layer of horsehair (see page 47).

13 Measure, cut out and set on the muslin (see page 48).

14 Lay on the cotton wadding (see page 48).

15 Measure, cut out and set on the top cover (see below).

16 Measure and cut outside panel (see page 61).

17 Make piping (see page 18).

18 Position piping with skewers (see page 62).

19 Stitch on top piping (see page 63).

20 Stitch panel to bottom piping (see page 63).

23 Finish with bottom cloth (see page 35).

POINTS TO REMEMBER

The first 14 stages of this project are building up a pad. Follow the instructions for the stuff-over bedroom chair (page 40) up to the point when you lay on the cotton wadding. Then follow stages 15–21 of the Order of Work given on the left, but bear the following points in mind:

• The webbing goes on top of the frame.

• When we tacked the scrim onto the bedroom chair, the frame was so delicate that we used ⅜-in. fine tacks. The chamfer on this footstool was broader, so we used ⅜-in. improved tacks.

BUILDING UP THE PAD FOR THE FOOTSTOOL

Don't be frightened by the size of this project. It is just a larger version of the stuff-over chair—and in some ways it is simpler, as you don't have the back uprights to contend with.

SETTING ON THE TOP COVER

Our original intention was to place the fabric so that the stripes ran lengthwise, but the age of this piece meant that one side was slightly warped, which would be accentuated by a lengthwise stripe. The warp was not evident, however, when we ran the stripes across. This is a good example of the importance of paying attention to the eccentricities of old furniture.

15(a) Lay the top-cover fabric on the frame, making sure that the stripes are straight. Measure and cut out. You don't need to allow for turning under, as you are going to tack onto the vertical edge and cover with a panel, but do allow extra fabric to grip onto, to pull it tight.

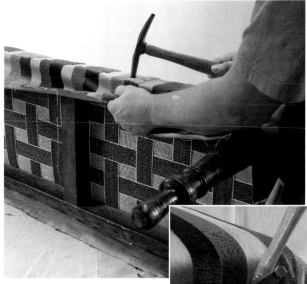

15(b) Temporary tack from side to side, and then from end to end. Inset: Tack on using ⅜-in. fine tacks, pulling the material tight as you work.

15(c) Trim off any surplus fabric. There is no need to tuck under the raw edges in this instance, as you are going to fit a piped panel of fabric over the top.

CUTTING SIDE PANEL

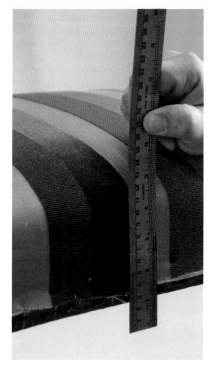

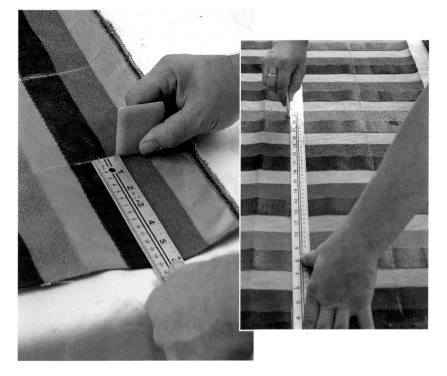

16(a) Measure the vertical side of the footstool to work out the depth for the piped panel, allowing about 1 in. (2.5 cm) extra to turn under at the top and and 1½ in. (4 cm) extra at the bottom to tack off on the underside.

16(b) Using tailor's chalk and a ruler, mark the depth of the panel on the fabric. (We used a contrasting color of chalk for the purposes of demonstration, but we recommend that you use a chalk that is close in color to your fabric.) Inset: Mark the length of the panel. You may need to cut several strips and join them together.

ATTACHING PIPING AND SIDE PANEL

The textural grandeur of this fabric would have overwhelmed most trims, although a bullion fringe might have done the job. We decided that the masculinity of the piece would be accentuated by piping at the top and bottom, giving it a square unity.

17 Make the piping (see page 18). You will need to sew several strips together to create a piece that is long enough to go all the way around. We chose a green stripe for the top piping and a purple stripe for the bottom.

18(a) Fix the green top piping at one corner with a loop pin, with the raw edge facing downward. Using a sliding bevel or a ruler to keep the piping straight, pin it around the top edge of the footstool side with long pins or loop pins.

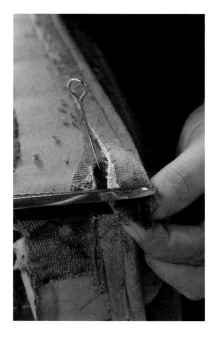

18(b) When you reach the starting point at which the two ends of the piping need to join, pin the piping into position.

18(c) Folding back the sleeve of tube of fabric around the piping cord, cut the cord about 1 in. (2.5 cm) back from the join.

18(d) Fold in the raw edge of the piping fabric tube so that it exactly meets the other end of the piping with no overlap. The double thickness of fabric will give the impression that there is cord inside.

18(e) Secure the join with loop pins.

18(f) Using a curved needle and waxed slipping thread, stitch the piping on with a locking-back stitch (see page 18).

19(a) Fold under one long raw edge of the side panel and pin on the side panel so that it butts up to the piping.

20 Tack the side border under the footstool. Then tack the raw edge of the piping under the footstool so that the piped side sits straight at the bottom. Neaten raw edges around the legs and use a hot glue gun to fix the piping in place.

21 Finish with the bottom cloth (see page 35).

19(b) Using a small curved needle and waxed slipping thread, slipstitch the side panel into position (see page 17). With this pattern, it was important to line up the stripes on the side with those on the top of the footstool. Whatever your pattern, aim to make it look as much as possible like a continuous piece of fabric.

Sprung dining chair

This chair may originally have been part of a set, but the detailed work of the splat, the cabriole legs and the ebonized finish make it a fine piece of furniture in its own right. We covered the seat in a taupe linen damask and embellished it with a cream pompom trim.

This project ushers in the use of springs, which work as an extra filling and base for the stuffed pad. We also introduce a goose-necked webbing stretcher, which makes it easier to protect the serpentine show-wood on the front of the chair.

TOOLS

Ripping chisel or staple remover
Mallet
Goose-neck webbing stretcher
Magnetic hammer
Tailor's shears
Tailor's chalk
Tape measure
5-in. 15-gauge curved needle
Regulator
Double-ended straight needle
Upholsterer's loop pins
Hot glue gun and glue sticks

MATERIALS

Tacks ⅝-in. improved, ½-in. improved, ⅜-in. improved, ⅜-in. fine
Black-and-white webbing
Springs
Italian hemp twine
10-oz burlap
3-ply jute cord
Horsehair
Linen scrim
Muslin
Cotton wadding
Top cover
Trimming
Bottom cloth

ORDER OF WORK

1 Strip (see page 26).

2 Position and fix the webbing (see page 66).

3 Make spring ties (see page 67).

4 Lash the springs with Italian hemp twine (see page 67).

5 Fix the burlap base and tie the springs to the burlap (see page 69).

6 Make stuffing ties (see page 30).

7 Stuff with horsehair (see page 31).

8 Set on the scrim (see page 42).

9 Stitch the bridle ties (see page 42).

10 Tack off the scrim (see page 43).

11 Regulate the stuffing (see page 43).

12 Blind stitch (see page 44).

13 Topstitch (see page 46).

14 Stuff with a second layer of horsehair (see page 47).

15 Measure, cut out and set on the muslin (see page 48).

16 Lay on the cotton wadding (see page 48).

17 Measure, cut out and set on the top cover (see page 70).

18 Attach the trim (see page 71).

19 Finish with the bottom cloth (see page 35).

THE ORIGINAL CHAIR
The original upholstery was in reasonable condition but we felt that the green-and-gold damask was not in harmony with the chair.

FIXING THE WEBBING

Begin by stripping (see page 26), then fix the webbing. The method of webbing for a sprung chair is the same as for the drop-in seat on page 26, but you need to stitch the springs to the webbing, so close interweaving is important.

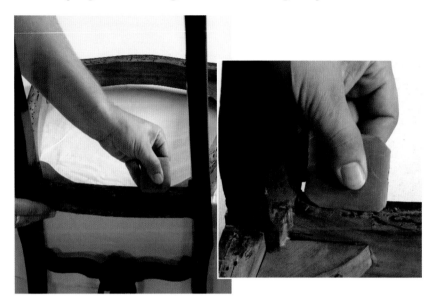

2(a) Using tailor's chalk, mark a line on the underside of the frame about ½ in. (1.25 cm) in from the edge as a guide to where to fix the webbing. You will later have to tack bottom cloth to cover the edges of the webbing.

2(b) Fold the end of the webbing, place it inside the chalked line and temporary tack three tacks near the fold.

2(c) Using a goose-necked webbing stretcher if you have one (see page 10), attach the webbing.

2(d) Secure each webbing strip with a W-formation of tacking (see page 26). Inset: Here, you can see the dense interweaving of the webbing needed to provide a base for the springs.

MAKING THE SPRING TIES

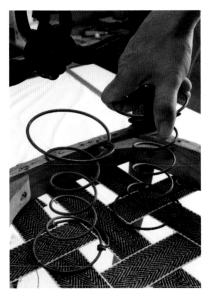

3(b) Draw around each spring with chalk to insure you are stitching it in the correct position. If possible, make sure that each spring is placed on a cross of webbing so that it is well supported underneath. Thread a curved needle with 3-ply jute cord and make a slip knot (see page 15) to secure the cord. Stitch over the spring as shown, then, on the underside, slip the needle through the loop to knot it. Sew three evenly spaced stitches around the bottom coil of each spring. Rotate the spring to make sure that it's not too loose. If it is, tighten your stitches.

Note: Reuse the springs whenever possible. However, if they are broken or twisted, replace them with springs of the same size and wire gauge.

3(a) We decided on four springs for this project, one set in from each corner. (A 2-in./5-cm gap between the springs is a good rule of thumb.) The fastened-off knot at the bottom of each spring should face inward, slightly away from the middle.

LASHING THE SPRINGS WITH TWINE

Lashing the springs with Italian hemp twine will tie them securely in place, ensuring that they move only vertically, not from side to side.

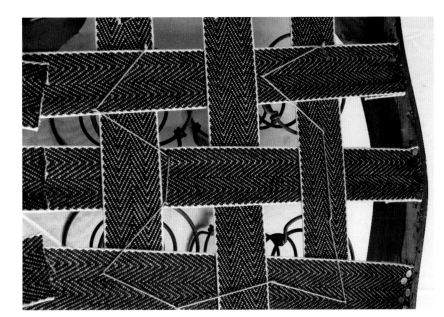

3(c) Don't fasten off until all the springs have been secured. The photo above shows the pattern of the cord on the underside.

4(a) Knock in two ⅝-in. improved tacks halfway on each side, in line with the springs. Cut Italian hemp twine roughly one-and-a-half times the length from rail to rail. Starting at the back righthand side, make a clove hitch knot (see page 14). Attach the twine to the back of the top coil, leaving a tail to fasten around the tack.

4(b) To secure the lashing, wind the twine around the tack, knock in, then knock another tack in next to it and wind the twine around that, forming a figure-of-eight with the twine looped around the tacks.

4(c) Knock in the tack and cut off the surplus twine.

4(d) Press the spring down vertically and make another clove hitch knot at the front of the coil, working toward the front. The spring's top coil should be lashed so that it is exactly over the bottom coil. Work the next spring in the same way. When you have lashed both springs, fasten off at the front in the same way that you secured the twine to start.

4(e) Work from back to front, from side to side and diagonally, knotting the twine in the center, as shown. This will prevent the burlap applied in the next stage from dipping in the middle.

FIXING THE BURLAP BASE

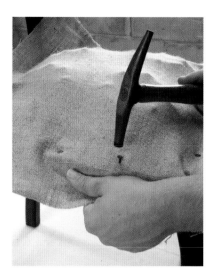

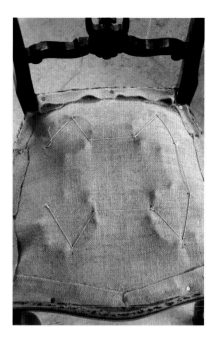

5(a) Cut 10-oz burlap to size, lay it over the springs and, using ½-in. improved tacks, tack into the middle of each rail, using the length of your thumb to pull the burlap taut. As always, tack from one side to the other to maintain tension.

5(b) Trim raw edges and fold the burlap inward, tacking to secure. Using a curved needle and 3-ply jute cord, stitch the burlap to the springs in a similar pattern to the one that you used to stitch the springs to the webbing.

5(c) The burlap will help to hold the springs in position, protect them from the horsehair, and provide a sturdy platform for the building of the stuffed pad, which is the next stage.

STUFFED PAD—BLIND STITCHING AND TOPSTITCHING

6–13 Follow the step-by-step instructions for the stuff-over bedroom chair on page 44–47, working from the point when you have set on your burlap base.

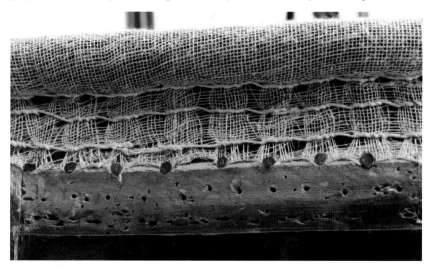

• You will need to make two rows of blind stitching and one row of topstitching.

• Remember to mark with tailor's chalk at 1-in. (2.5-cm) intervals to keep your stitches even. The picture shows how the threads of the scrim clump together with even stitching. Work the first row of blind stitching just above the tacks.

• When working the topstitch, remember to keep regulating to keep the top roll firm and full.

STUFFING TIES, SECOND STUFFING, MUSLIN, AND COTTON WADDING

14–16 Work these stages in the same way as the drop-in seat on page 24. As this chair has a pad beneath, also refer to the bedroom chair (page 47), following the steps after building the stuffed-over pad.

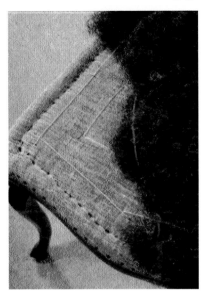

• Work the stuffing ties in two squares, with a line down the middle from front to back, as shown in the photo on the left.

• Fill with a second layer of horsehair, teasing it out and feeling with your hands to check that it is uniformly thick and even.

• Use loop pins to secure the muslin before you tack.

• Use two layers of cotton wadding, paper side up. There's no need to tack, but trim to just above the show-wood.

TOP COVER

An opulent taupe linen damask was just perfect for the top cover of this chair. The large, light pattern brought out the small detailing on the back of the chair without fighting with it and contrasted well with the ebonized finish.

17(a) Lay out the cloth to look for the exact section of pattern that you want on the seat.

17(b) When we looked at the toile de Jouy for the drop-in seat, we looked for a pattern to center on the pad. With this chair, we found a shape that echoes the detailing on the back—a wide pattern at the front, narrowing to a small flower at the base of the ornate panel in the back of the chair, which opens out at the top. This connects the frame with the fabric and draws the eye over the chair as a whole.

17(c) Centering from front to back is very important. The small flower needed to be positioned centrally toward the back, in line with the bottom of the splat, without slipping over the back of the pad and out of view. Temporary tack until you are satisfied that the top cover is correctly positioned. Refer to the step-by-step instructions for the stuff-over pad for the bedroom chair (page 48) and pay particular attention to the corners.

TRIMMING

The pompom trim picks up the berry motif in the pattern and adds a light and frivolous touch without overpowering the effect.

18 Glue on the trim in the same way as for the pin-stuffed chair (page 36) and the stuff-over pad for the bedroom chair (page 40). Make sure the pompoms are hanging down and don't get glue on them.

19 Finish with the bottom cloth (see page 35).

Blanket box

Adorn your bedroom with this gorgeous lined blanket box. It hides quantities of clutter, provides a comfortable place to sit, and gives you the opportunity to introduce a fabric that you adore to your decorating scheme. For such an impressive piece it's a very easy project, and one that you can create from scratch at surprisingly little cost.

Unless your joinery skills are particularly good, buy your frame from an upholstery frame supplier. The upholstered pad on the lid is constructed with a stuff-over pad in just the same way as the long footstool (page 58) and the stuff-over bedroom chair (page 40). For setting on the top cover, refer to the steps for covering the stuff-over bedroom chair. This project introduces the use of blind-tacking strip.

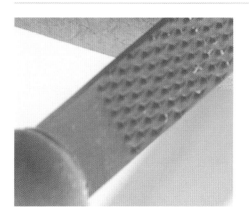

TOOLS

Sandpaper, plane or rasp
Magnetic hammer
Tailor's shears
Tape measure
Tailor's chalk
Pins
Small curved needle
Webbing stretcher
Double-ended straight needle
Regulator
5-in. 15-gauge curved needle
Screwdriver

MATERIALS

Beech frame
7-oz burlap
Tacks: ⅜-in. improved, ⅜-in. fine
Cotton felt
Cotton wadding
Top cover
Gimp pins
Waxed slipping thread
Cotton sateen curtain lining
Blind-tacking strip
Black-and-white webbing
10-oz burlap
Horsehair
Linen scrim
Muslin
2 hinges
4 felted glide feet

THE FRAME
The empty sides of this beech frame will be filled with layers of upholstery. A solid wooden frame would make a box of this size impossibly heavy.

ORDER OF WORK

Work the lid and box separately.

1 Chamfer the edges of the frame (see below).

BOX

2 Fix 7-oz burlap to the four sides, but not to the top or the bottom (see below).

LONG SIDES

3 Lay cotton felt over the burlap (see page 75).

4 Tack the cotton wadding into position (see page 75).

5 Set on the top cover (see page 75).

SHORT SIDES

6 Cover the burlap with cotton felt. Tack the cotton wadding in position (see page 76).

7 Pin the top cover in position (see page 76).

8 Fold the top corners (see page 76).

9 Adjust the pins, tack over the top and bottom and slipstitch the top cover into position (see page 76).

LINING FOR ALL FOUR SIDES

10 Cut and measure the lining fabric and tack on the lining (see page 77).

11 Tack on the cotton wadding (see page 77).

12 Tack on blind-tacking strip (see page 77).

13 Fold the lining into the box (see page 77).

14 Using blind-tacking strip, tack the lining to the base (see page 78).

BASE BOARD

15 Tack on cotton wadding, cover with lining fabric and set in the base board (see page 78).

LID

16 Make a stuff-over pad and set on the top cover (see pages 26–31 and 42–48), then slipstitch (see page 17) the lining fabric to the bottom of the lid.

ASSEMBLING THE BLANKET BOX

17 Fix the lid to the box with two hinges (see page 78).

18 Make the stays (see page 79).

19 Attach the stays with gimp pins (see page 79).

20 Finish with bottom cloth (see page 35) and attach four felted glide feet.

PREPARING THE FRAME

1 Chamfer the edges of the frame using sandpaper, a plane or a rasp. A softer edge is less likely to wear the fabric.

2 Line the four sides of the box, but not the top or bottom, with 7-oz burlap and fix in place with ⅜-in. improved tacks; the broad heads will hold the open weave firmly. Tack in the center of each side, folding the raw edges under and using the selvage if possible. Work out from the center, tacking from side to side and stretching the burlap to keep it taut.

SETTING ON THE BURLAP

The burlap is not load bearing, so a lightweight (7-oz) burlap will suffice.

LONG SIDES: COTTON FELT, COTTON WADDING, TOP COVER

Deal with the front then the back panel (the long sides).

3 Lay cotton felt on the front panel and remove the brown paper. Don't cut the felt, as this will give too defined an edge and blunt your shears; instead, lay one hand flat on the felt at the edge of the rail and use your other hand to pull away the excess, so that the felt is flush with the edge of the panel.

4 Cut the cotton wadding to size, allowing a small overhang all around, and lay it on the cotton felt. Using ⅜-in. improved tacks, tack the cotton wadding around the side rails. Tack under the bottom of the box and fold the cotton wadding around the top rail to tack onto the underside.

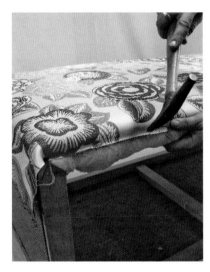

5(a) Measure and cut the top cover, allowing extra to fold over and around the top rail, under the bottom rail and around the sides. Using ⅜-in. fine tacks, temporary tack the cover in place, then knock in the tacks along the side rails. Along the bottom, pull the fabric under the box and tack. Along the top, pull the fabric over the top rail and tack along the underside of the top rail. Do not tack onto the top of the box as this will wear through the fabric.

5(b) Tack the corners neatly. You don't need to fold under any of the raw edges, as they will be concealed.

5(c) The edge and the sides of the completed front panel should look like this. Now cover the back panel in the same way.

SHORT SIDES AND CORNERS:
COTTON FELT, COTTON WADDING, TOP COVER

6 The side panels are covered with cotton felt and cotton wadding, in exactly the same way as for the long panels. Then you need to cut and fix the top cover: the cutting instructions for the top cover are slightly different from the front and back panels, as you need to allow extra fabric for slipstitching. You need to miter the corners on the top rail for a really neat finish. It is rarely possible to match exactly the sections of an asymmetrically-patterned fabric, but do try to line up its most prominent features.

7(a) Cut the fabric for the side panels to size, adding enough extra to allow for folding the fabric around the top rail and to tack under the box, plus about ½ in. (1.25 cm) on the sides to fold under for slipstitching. Temporary tack along the bottom rail, using ⅜-in. fine tacks.

7(b) Pin at the corners, folding the raw edges neatly under.

8 Along the top rail, fold back the corner and cut off the point.

9 Fold the fabric under to make a mitered corner and tack neatly with gimp pins in a coordinating color. Pull against this fixing to tack the fabric under the top rail. Then pull downward, adjusting your pins to take out any fullness and retacking at the bottom if necessary. Slipstitch into position (see page 17).

LINING

Now, with the bottom board in place (not the base board, which will be placed later), turn the box on its side. Here we introduce blind-tacking strip. This is a thin strip of stiff card, which is tacked on to give a straight edge when fabric is folded over it. We use it to give a neat join between the lining and the top cover at the top of the box. We also use it in the bottom of the box, to hold the lining flat against the sides.

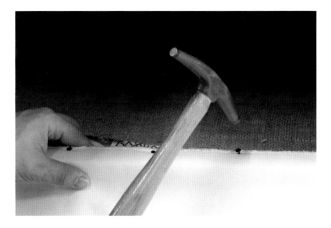

10 Measure the inside front of the box and add about 5 in. (12 cm) to the height to allow for tacking the lining onto the bottom of the box, and for tacking on at the top. Add an extra 2 in. (5 cm) to the width to allow for folding the fabric under at the sides. Cut your lining fabric to this measurement. Lay it out facing you, with the wrong side uppermost. Using ⅜-in. fine tacks, tack it onto the inside edge of the top rail. Use only a few tacks.

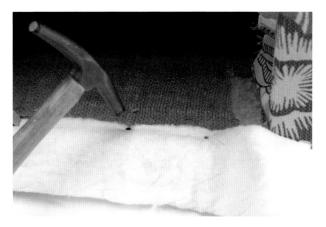

11 Fold a length of cotton wadding, paper side up, to the length of the blanket box and about 4 in. (10 cm) deep. Using ⅜-in. fine tacks, tack the cotton wadding onto the inside edge of the top rail. Again, use only a few tacks. This will soften the cardboard edge of the blind-tacking strip.

12 On the same tack line, using ⅜-in. fine tacks, tack a length of blind-tacking strip. This will give a neat, straight edge. Make sure that the tacks are closer to the folding edge, so that the card doesn't bend when you fold the fabric over. Tack at 1-in. (2.5-cm) intervals.

13 Fold the lining fabric and cotton wadding into the box. Repeat on the other three sides. Temporary tack the fabric onto the bottom of the box.

14(a) In the bottom of the box, pull the fabric taut and tack blind-tacking strip along the edges to anchor the lining. This avoids tack ties (pulls in the fabric made by tacks) and gives a clean edge.

14(b) Carefully trim off any surplus lining that sticks out beyond the blind-tacking strip. Fold the raw edges under. The fabric is taut enough to dispense with stitching. Trim off the excess.

BASE BOARD

15 The base board is set into the box after the lining has been fixed and should be slightly smaller than the box opening. Cover it with a layer of cotton wadding and lining fabric. Tack the cotton wadding and lining fabric onto the underside of the base board.

THE LID

16 The pad on the lid frame is constructed in exactly the same way as for the stuff-over bedroom chair (pages 42–48) and the long footstool (page 58. Cover in the same way as for the stuff-over chair, but note the following points:

• Pull the cotton wadding, muslin, and top cover under the frame, and tack.

• The raw edges of the top cover do not need not be tacked under.

• On the underside, slipstitch a lining of cotton sateen.

FIXING THE HINGES

Once you've made a stuff-over pad for the lid and set on the top cover, you can fix the lid to the box.

17 Fix two hinges on top of the fabric. If you attempt to set them in, the lid will not close properly. Measure in from the edge of the lid and box to insure the two parts of the hinge align. Stick pins through the screw holes to mark the screw positions.

MAKING AND ATTACHING THE STAYS

Sturdy fabric stays will prevent the lid falling from backward. The stays should be 1 in. (2.5 cm) wide; the length will depend on the size of your box. Experiment with a piece of webbing until you arrive at the best length.

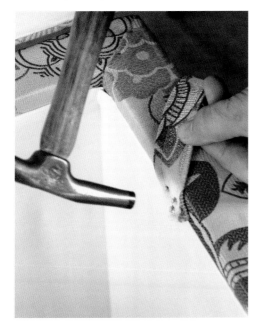

18 Cut a piece of top-cover fabric to the required length for the stays and about 2½ in. (6 cm) wide. Fold in the raw edges, then fold in half lengthwise and machine stitch through both layers, stitching up each side and across the top and bottom. Set the angle of the lid so that it doesn't fall too far back or fall shut. Fix one end of each stay in a side rail, using four gimp pins.

19 Turn the other end of each stay so that it faces to the edge of the lid and fix with gimp pins. This arrangement means that the stay will neatly fold into the box when you close the lid.

20 Finish with the bottom cloth (see page 35) and fix four felted glide feet in the corners.

Padded silk headboard

Fabulous in brilliant fuchsia, reminiscent in shape and hue of Mae West's lips, this padded silk headboard started life as a large sheet of plywood from a building supply depot.

This is one of the quickest, easiest and cheapest projects in this book. If you own or can borrow a jigsaw, it is a simple task to cut out the headboard—and the upholstery is nothing more than a pin-stuffing job on a large scale.

Refer back to the techniques used to upholster the pin-stuffed chair (page 36) and to the blanket box lining (page 77) for how to use blind-tacking strip. This project also gives tips on upholstering with a delicate fabric.

TOOLS

Jigsaw
Magnetic hammer
Tailor's shears
Yardstick
Tailor's chalk
Pencil
5-in. 15-gauge curved needle
Regulator

MATERIALS

Good furniture-grade plywood
10-oz burlap
Tacks: ⅜-in. improved, ⅜-in. fine
3-ply jute cord
Horsehair
Muslin
Cotton wadding
Blind-tacking strip
Top cover
Bottom cloth or lining fabric

ORDER OF WORK

1 Measure your bed, cut the plywood to shape and mark the mattress line (see page 82).

ABOVE THE MATTRESS LINE

2 Fix the burlap (see page 82).

3 Make stuffing ties (see pages 30 and 82).

4 Stuff with horsehair (see pages 31 and 82).

5 Cover with muslin (see page 83).

6 Lay on cotton wadding (see page 83).

7 Measure, cut out and set on the top cover (see page 84).

8 Fold the corners (see page 34).

BELOW THE MATTRESS LINE

9 Measure and cut out the top cover and tear off cotton wadding to size (see page 85).

10 Using blind-tacking strip, tack over the cotton wadding and the top cover (see page 77).

11 Fold the top cover and cotton wadding over and under the bottom edge, and tack and fold the corners (see pages 77 and 78).

BACK OF THE HEADBOARD

12 Cover the back with lining, muslin or bottom cloth (see page 35).

THE UNPADDED HEADBOARD
It's hard to believe that a sheet of plywood, which at this stage is rather reminiscent of a farmyard gate, will become the sleek, silk headboard pictured opposite.

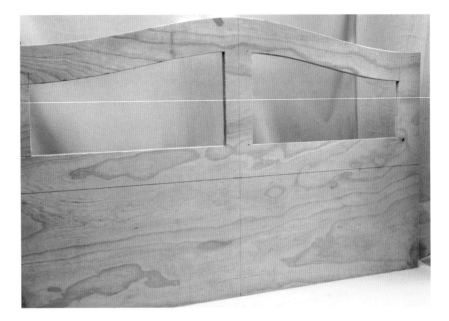

MEASURING, CUTTING, AND MARKING THE PLY

Measure the distance from the floor to the top of the mattress, then measure the height of the headboard that you want above the mattress. Buy furniture-grade plywood from a building supply depot, and having drawn on the shape you want, cut out with a jigsaw. Take out two panels. This allows you to set on the burlap to make the stuffing ties and also makes the headboard lighter.

1 Draw a line where you want the stuffing to end. This will be where the top pin-stuffed section reaches the mattress.

ABOVE THE MATTRESS LINE

The headboard is worked in two stages. Above the mattress line, it is well padded to provide cushioning and comfort. Below, it is worked as flat as possible so that it lies flush against the wall behind the bed.

FIXING THE BURLAP

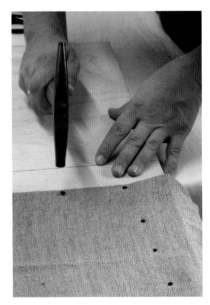

2 Using ⅜-in. improved tacks, tack on 10-oz burlap to cover the open panels, leaving about 2 in. (5 cm) of plywood all around. Start tacking in the center and work outward. Fold under the raw edges and tack down.

MAKING STUFFING TIES

3 Make stuffing ties (see page 30) in the pattern shown in the photo above.

STUFFING WITH HORSEHAIR

4 Stuff with horsehair, keeping it up to the edge but rolling it in so that it doesn't creep over the edge, which would give your headboard a lumpy profile—not at all glamorous.

COVER WITH MUSLIN

5(a) Cut the muslin to size, allowing an extra 3 in. (7.5 cm) to fold over at the top and ½ in. (1.25 cm) extra to fold under at the bottom. Using ⅜-in. fine tacks, tack the muslin across the bottom of the pad above the mattress line, leaving room to tack on the top cover.

5(b) Pull the muslin up over the back and tack into position. Pull the muslin around the sides and tack.

LAYING ON THE COTTON WADDING

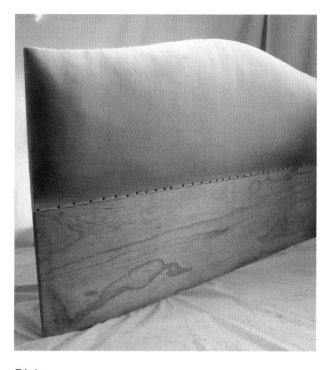

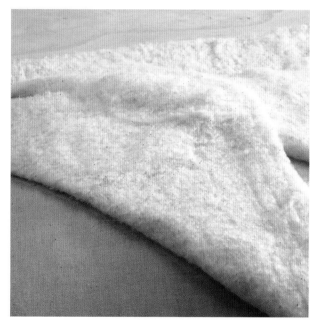

5(c) Tack all around, smoothing the pad upward and outward with your hand as you work. It is important that the muslin has a smooth finish. The silk needs to be laid on rather than stretched. It is a delicate fabric and will tear if it is handled roughly.

6 Lay on two layers of cotton wadding to cover the muslin, taking it over the back of the frame and around the sides. This will protect the top cover from wear. Using ⅜-in. fine tacks, tack the cotton wadding into position.

CUTTING AND SETTING ON THE TOP COVER

The sheen and light-reflecting nature of silk mean that you must exercise extreme caution with your tacking. Even with the slightest pull, each tack can produce a noticeable line in the fabric (called a tack tie), which will catch the light.

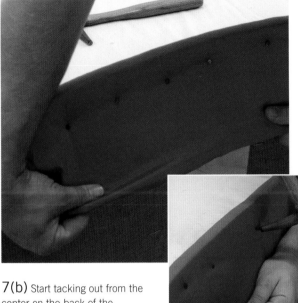

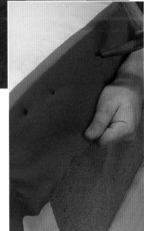

7(a) Measure and cut out the top-cover fabric to come down as far as the top of the mattress, allowing an extra 3 in. (7.5 cm) to fold over at the top and ½ in. (1.25 cm) at the bottom—unless you can use the selvage and don't have to fold the edge under. Starting at the mattress line, make a pencil mark every 2 in. (5 cm) on the ply and tack the top-cover fabric accordingly. Knock in three ⅜-in. fine tacks in the center of the bottom edge, then pull the fabric over the top and temporary tack into the back of the headboard to hold it in position. Pull gently and smooth. Finish tacking the bottom edge.

7(b) Start tacking out from the center on the back of the headboard, smoothing the fabric upward and sideways with the flat of your hand. Tack at least 2 in. (5 cm) down from the top of the headboard to minimize the risk of pulls showing on the front. Tack out from the center.

FOLD IN THE CORNERS

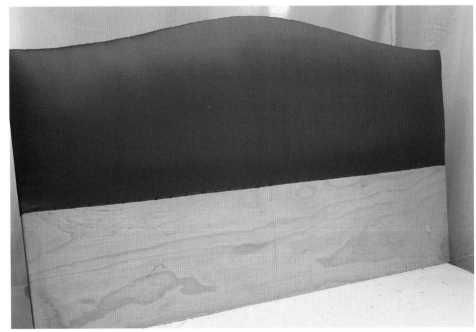

8 Temporary tack the top-cover fabric around the sides of the headboard. Fold in the corners in the same way as for the dining chair drop-in seat (page 34). When you are happy with the positioning, drive the tacks home.

BELOW THE MATTRESS LINE MEASURE AND CUT THE TOP COVER

The use of blind-tacking strip will provide a neat contrast, delineating the end of the stuffed pad. A sharp line is particularly important when using silk, as any slight wrinkle will catch the light. Attention to detail is the sign of a good upholsterer although, admittedly, pillows will usually hide this area.

9 Measure and cut out the top cover to fit the exposed plywood, with enough extra to tuck under the bottom, around the sides, and over the top. Tear off a piece of cotton wadding to fit the explosed plywood. Use only one layer. This section will tuck down behind the mattress and you need to minimize bulk. Lay the top cover, wrong side up, and then the cotton wadding, furry side up, over the stuffed pad, with the bottom edges below the tack line.

10 As with the blanket box lining (page 77), use blind-tacking strip to achieve a straight, sharp line. Place the blind-tacking strip above the tack line. Using a ruler or sliding bevel to keep it straight and starting in the middle, tack the blind-tacking strip in place with ⅜-in. fine tacks.

11 Turn the headboard upside down and rest it on something clean. Fold the cotton wadding and top cover back over the exposed plywood. Using ⅜-in. fine tacks, tack the cotton wadding and top cover in place on the back of the headboard, folding in the corners (see page 34).

COVERING THE BACK

12 Finish by tacking on lining fabric (muslin, bottom cloth or sateen curtain lining) to cover the back.

Gilded chair

This gilded chair, with its rounded back and lovely squat shape, came from a brocante near Limoges in Southwest France. The frame was tatty, but traditionally gilded with gold leaf on gesso. Gold paint is a poor substitute. The gold-and-red silk of the upholstery was torn and frayed beyond repair and leaking hay stuffing.

We decided to take the middle path between restoration and conservation. We saved the pads and chose a sleek black fabric with raised chenille dots, which contrasted beautifully with the chipped and worn gilt, enhancing the qualities of each.

This project introduces upholstering the back of a chair, reusing old materials, and upholstering arm pads.

TOOLS

Ripping chisel or staple remover
Mallet
Webbing stretcher
Tailor's shears
Tailor's chalk
Tape measure
Magnetic hammer
Double-ended straight needle
Pins
Small curved needle
Upholsterer's loop pins
Hot glue gun and
 glue sticks

MATERIALS

Tacks ½-in. improved, ⅜-in. improved,
 ⅜-in. fine
3-ply jute cord
Black-and-white webbing
10-oz burlap
Horsehair
Linen scrim
Muslin
Waxed slipping thread
Cotton wadding
Springs
Italian hemp twine
Top cover
Braid
Bottom cloth

THE ORIGINAL CHAIR
The gold-and-red silk upholstery was beyond repair, but the pads were in good condition.

ORDER OF WORK

1 Strip (see page 26).

BACK

2 Position and fix the webbing (see pages 26 and 88).

3 Fix the burlap base (see page 89).

4 Reuse the original pad (see page 89).

5 Set on the scrim (see page 90).

6 Make a locking-back stitch (see page 90).

7 Tack off the scrim (see page 90).

8 Topstitch (see page 46).

9 Make the stuffing ties (see page 30).

10 Stuff with horsehair (see page 31).

11 Attach the muslin (see page 91).

SEAT

12 Position and fix the webbing (see page 66).

13 Make the spring ties (see page 67).

14 Lash the springs with Italian hemp twine (see page 67).

BACK

15 Lay on the cotton wadding (see page 32).

16 Measure, cut out and set on the top cover (see page 33).

OUTSIDE BACK PANEL

17 Cut out, position and tack on the muslin (see pages 32 and 92).

18 Lay on the cotton wadding (see pages 32 and 92).

19 Measure, cut out and set on the top cover (see pages 33 and 92).

SEAT

20 Fix the burlap base (see pages 28 and 69).

21 Tie the springs to the burlap base (see page 69).

22 Reuse the old pad (see page 89).

23 Set on the scrim (see page 42).

24 Stitch the bridle ties (see page 42).

25 Tack off the scrim (see page 43).

26 Blind stitch (see page 44).

27 Topstitch (see page 46).

28 Make the stuffing ties (see page 30).

29 Stuff with a second layer of horsehair (see page 47).

30 Set on the muslin (see page 48).

31 Lay on the cotton wadding (see page 48).

32 Measure, cut out and set on the top cover (see page 48).

ARM PADS

33 Make the stuffing ties (see pages 30 and 54).

34 Stuff with horsehair (see page 31).

35 Cut out, position and tack on the muslin (see page 32) and regulate the stuffing (see page 43).

36 Lay on the cotton wadding (see page 32).

37 Measure, cut out and set on the top cover (see page 33).

WHOLE CHAIR

38 Attach the trim (see page 38).

39 Finish with the bottom cloth (see page 35).

BACK

FIXING THE WEBBING

2 Normally we would have put a cross of webbing on the back of a chair like this, but you have to take account of the vagaries of old furniture. Because the subframe was so thin at the sides, we used three vertical webs at the back. Inset: Because of the sub-frame, we had to place the tacks holding the webbing close together, but we used the usual W-formation—albeit a shallow W. Use ⅜-in. improved tacks if you have a shallow rail.

FIXING THE BURLAP BASE

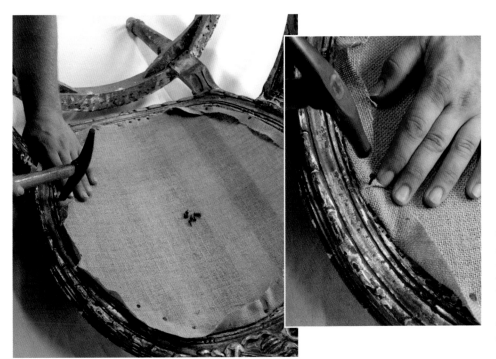

3 Cut the burlap to shape. Using ⅜-in. improved tacks, tack it tightly from top to bottom onto the sub frame, then lay it on from side to side so that it follows the curve of the back of the chair. Trim the rough edges, leaving about 1 in. (2.5 cm) overlap, then fold over the overlap and tack down.

REUSING THE ORIGINAL PAD

4(a) If you can salvage the original pad, it will save you a lot of work. Set the pad in position. Inset: You may find it easier to lay the chair on its back.

4(b) Tie the pad to the webbing in the center using a double-ended needle and a slip knot (see page 15).

SETTING ON
THE SCRIM

5 The scrim will hold the pad in place. Cut the scrim to size and lay it over the pad. Using a double-ended needle and 3-ply jute cord, make a slip knot at the center of the pad at the bottom.

TOPSTITCHING AND
SECOND STUFFING

MAKING A LOCKING-BACK STITCH

Locking-back stitch is used to secure a pad to the base burlap, particularly on the backs of chairs. It usually runs down the center of the pad.

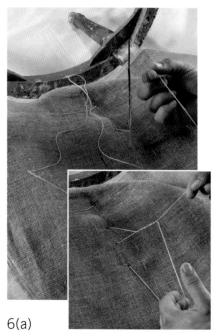

6(a)
Stitch up the middle using a locking-back stitch. This works like blind stitch and topstitch. In a similar way, you work backstitch and twist the cord three times around the needle.

6(b) and 7 Fold under the edges of the scrim and, using ⅜-in. improved tacks, tack down.

8 Using the original roll as a guide, topstitch as you did with the stuff-over bedroom chair (page 46) and the sprung dining chair (page 69), to set the pad in position and bring out the top roll.

9 and 10 Make a spiral of stuffing ties. Lay the chair down to stuff the back with horsehair, pressing down to feel for any clumps. Be sure that the horsehair fits snugly up to the roll.

ATTACHING THE MUSLIN

11(a) Cut the muslin to size and pin it onto the top of the roll, turning under the raw edges. Inset: Use plenty of pins. We decided to sew the muslin to minimize bulky tack fixing in this fine frame. This is also a useful technique if your tack wood is overworked and full of holes.

11(b) Using a small curved needle and waxed slipping thread, slipstitch the muslin in place, removing the pins as you work. Pick up a few threads of burlap on the fold of the muslin, just behind your last stitch, then slip the needle into the fold of the muslin. As the needle emerges, pick up a couple of threads of burlap behind and continue. Slipstitches should not be seen.

11(c) Take out any remaining pins.

SEAT SPRUNG BASE

12–14 The principles of making the sprung base are the same as for the sprung dining chair (see pages 66–68), but the upholstered back and shape of the seat demand a different pattern for the springs.

- We reused the six springs that we found in the chair.

- The wide front called for three springs—one in the center and one at each corner.

- The back of the seat narrows and slopes slightly to accommodate the upholstered back. We put one spring in each corner and one spring in the middle of the chair.

BACK TOP COVER

15–16 With the springs lashed into place, this is the moment to set the top cover on the back of the chair. If you start to build up your seat pad first, you will find that you have limited room to work.

- Lay the chair on its back.
- Work much as you did to set the top cover on the pin-stuffed chair (see page 33), bearing in mind the tips for dealing with a round pad that you learnt while upholstering the piano stool (page 56–57).
- Cut a double layer of cotton wadding to shape. Use a few tacks to keep it in place.
- Measure and cut out the top cover.
- Set the top cover on, turning the edges under, and temporary tack it in place at the top and bottom, then at each side.
- Keep working from one side to the other, evening out puckers and smoothing out fullness.

OUTSIDE BACK PANEL

The back panel is made up of a layer of muslin, a layer of cotton wadding, then the top cover. It is easier to work if you lay the chair on its front.

17 Tack on the muslin using ⅜-in. fine tacks. Make sure you tack the muslin close to the inside edge, to give you room to tack on the top cover.

18 Lay on a double layer of cotton wadding and tack sparingly to hold it in place.

19 Measure and cut out the top cover. Mark the center point at the bottom and top of the chair with chalk and make notches in the corresponding center of the fabric. Keep the notches in line with the chalk marks. Temporary tack, using ⅜-in. fine tacks. Make sure the pattern is straight, then drive the tacks home

SEAT BURLAP, PAD, SCRIM, BRIDLE TIES.

BLIND STITCHING AND TOPSTITCHING

20–25 Using the same method as the sprung dining chair, cover the springs with 10-oz burlap. As you did with the back of the chair, set on the old pad and cover it with scrim, attaching it to the burlap with bridle ties as shown above. Tack on the scrim, leaving a margin of tack wood to tack on the top cover (see pages 67–70).

26 While working the seat, be aware of the slope at the back of the seat which has no top-roll and does not need stitching.

27 Topstitch through the scrim to follow the existing topstitching in the pad. Work one row of blind stitching to bring the pad toward the edge of the frame. The pad is already blind stitched to give it shape.

STUFFING TIES, HORSEHAIR, AND MUSLIN

28–29 Make the stuffing ties and stuff with a second layer of horsehair, following the instructions for the stuff-over bedroom chair (see pages 30–31).

30(a) Stitch on the muslin in the same way as for the back of the chair. Tuck the edge of the muslin under the horsehair and pin the fold at the edge, just on top of the roll, with loop pins.

30(b) Sew the muslin in place using slipstitch.

TOP COVER

31 and 32 Lay on the cotton wadding and cover the pad, following the guidelines for the stuff-over bedroom chair (page 48–49)and the sprung dining chair (page 70). Treat the cuts for the front legs in the same way as the back legs.

ARM PADS

33 To make the stuffing ties on the arm pads, knock a ½-in. improved tack in halfway at each end of the arm pad (see Victorian piano stool, page 54). Tie 3-ply jute cord onto the tacks to make a loop that you can fit three fingers under. Drive the tacks in to secure the cord.

34 Stuff horsehair through the loop, rolling and tucking it under with your hands so that it sits on top of the arm.

35(a) Cut out, position and tack on the muslin to cover the horsehair (you can use small off-cuts of muslin here).

35(b) Using ⅜-in. fine tacks, temporary tack the muslin at each end.

35(c) Use the flat of the regulator to prevent the stuffing from slipping down the sides. Knock in the tacks.

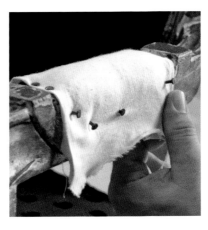

35(d) Temporary tack the muslin at the lowest point on either side, keeping well clear of the show wood. Temporary tack all around, then knock in the tacks.

35(e) Trim the muslin.

TRIMMING

36 and 37(a) Use two layers of cotton wadding, trim to shape, then cut out and set on the top cover. This is the perfect opportunity to use up scraps. With this fabric, we positioned a dot at the center of each end of the arm pad and tacked the fabric in place. Although the arm is slightly serpentine, fixing the pattern in a straight line on the arm pad gives the best effect.

37(b) Tack the top cover on the arm pads, turning under as you go.

38 Attach the trimming (see page 38). We chose a black trimming that suits the sexiness of this chair. Don't forget to trim the back panel.

39 Finish with the bottom cloth (see page 35).

Nursing chair

This little Victorian nursing chair was covered in a brownish sprigged pattern, which managed to seem both drab and fussy. The gorgeously scrolled woodwork was dull, and the upholstery sagged and looked well worn.

We chose a simple dotted fabric, which gave the chair a fresh, light appearance without compromising its Victorian origins, and waxed the beautiful rosewood frame to a soft glow.

This project introduces buttoning, which looks stunning and is surprisingly straightforward. There is nothing complicated about the seat, which is a sprung, stuff-over pad like the bedroom chair (page 40) and the gilded chair (page 86).

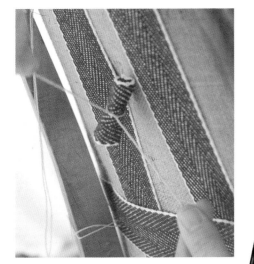

TOOLS

Ripping chisel or staple remover
Mallet
Webbing stretcher
Magnetic hammer
Tailor's shears
Tailor's chalk and tape measure
5-in. 15-gauge curved needle
Regulator and wooden pleating tool
Double-ended straight needle
Sewing machine
Hot glue gun and glue sticks

MATERIALS

Tacks: ½-in. improved, ⅜-in. improved, ⅜-in. fine
3-ply jute cord
Black-and-white webbing
10-oz burlap
Horsehair
Linen scrim
Cotton felt
Buttons
Muslin
Cotton wadding
Top cover
Piping cord
Gimp pins
Bottom cloth

THE ORIGINAL CHAIR
Under the shabby upholstery was a beautiful little chair, just waiting to be discovered.

STRIPPING AND PREPARING THE FRAME

1 We found nothing to save when we stripped this chair, so our project started from scratch. Before we began recovering, we waxed the show-wood and discovered just how pretty the rosewood was once its warm, brown tones were softly glowing.

ORDER OF WORK

1 Strip (see page 26) and wax the show-wood.

BACK

2 Position and fix the webbing and the burlap base (see pages 26–29 and below).

3 Make the stuffing ties, stuff with horsehair and set on the scrim (see pages 30–31, 42 and below).

4 Make bridle ties (see page 42).

5 Tack off the scrim (see page 43).

6 Regulate the stuffing to the edge for the top-stitch roll (see page 43).

7 Topstitch (see page 46).

8 Make stuffing ties (see page 30).

9 Make second stuffing (see page 47).

10 Tack on a layer of cotton felt and a double layer of cotton wadding (see page 75).

BUTTONING

11 Measure to find the center (see page 99).

12 Position the buttons and mark with a tack (see page 99).

13 Removing markers, make a hole through to the scrim (see page 99).

14 Measure and cut out the top cover, adding an extension of muslin if you wish (see page 100).

15 Lay on the top cover without tacking (see page 100).

16 Make button ties (see page 100).

17 Neaten the pleats (see page 100).

18 Tack on the top cover (see page 101).

19 Tie in buttons (see page 101).

20 Check the pleats again (see page 101).

SEAT

21 Position and fix the webbing (see page 26).

22 Make the spring ties (see page 67).

23 Lash the springs with Italian hemp twine (see page 67).

24 Fix the burlap base (see page 69).

25 Tie the springs to the burlap base (see page 69).

26 Make stuffing ties (see page 30).

27 Stuff with horsehair (see page 31).

28 Set on the scrim (see page 42).

29 Stitch the bridle ties (see page 42.

30 Tack off the scrim (see page 43).

31 Regulate the stuffing (see page 43).

32 Blind stitch (see page 44).

33 Topstitch (see page 46).

34 Stuff with a second layer of horsehair (see page 47).

35 Measure, cut out and set on the muslin (see page 48).

36 Lay on the cotton wadding (see page 48).

37 Measure, cut out and set on the top cover (see page 48).

OUTSIDE BACK PANEL

38 Tack on the muslin (see page 102).

39 Lay on the cotton wadding (see page 103).

40 Measure, cut out and set on the top cover (see page 48).

41 Slipstitch the top edge to the back of the top roll, then tack the lower edge and the sides (see page 103).

WHOLE CHAIR

42 Make double piping (see page 19).

43 Attach the double piping (see page 103).

44 Finish with the bottom cloth (see page 35).

BACK FIXING THE WEBBING AND BURLAP

2 Using ½-in. improved tacks, tack on four upright webs, two either side of the central back vertical rail, and tack one web across the middle. Stretch 10-oz burlap from top to bottom, but lay it from side to side in order to maintain the curve of the back. Temporary tack the burlap in place, then tack down with ⅜-in. improved tacks.

STUFFING TIES, HORSEHAIR, AND SCRIM

3–6 Make the stuffing ties into a sort of square spiral. Stuff to a compressed depth of about 1 in. (2.5 cm) thick. If the horsehair is too deep, the buttons will sink into it out of sight. The scrim should be stretched from top to bottom and laid over from side to side, held in place with temporary tacks. As with the gilded chair (page 90), make a line of bridle ties up the middle anchoring the center of the stuffing to the burlap base. Folding raw edges under the horsehair, tack the scrim into position with ⅜-in. improved tacks.

TOPSTITCHING

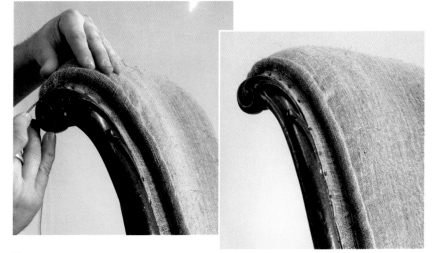

7 Regulate a good supply of stuffing to the edge before you start topstitching. Don't stint on the regulator as you stitch. Topstitch around the edge, using a 5-in. 15-gauge curved needle, which is easier to use in this case than the double-ended straight needle because the side rail is so close and prominent. Otherwise, the method is the same.

MAKING THE SECOND STUFFING

8–9 Make stuffing ties in a right angle zigzag of about four horizontals, depending on the size of the chair. Don't make the second stuffing too thick and keep the edge of the stuffing on the top-stitched roll.

COTTON FELT, COTTON WADDING, AND MAKING THE HOLES FOR BUTTONS

10 Set on a layer of cotton felt, remembering to remove the brown paper and to tear, rather than cut, the edges (see page 75). Tack on a double layer of cotton wadding over the top, using ⅜-in. fine tacks.

11 We followed the chair's original button positioning—three at the top and bottom and two in the center. Remember that the seat pad will obscure the lower section, so don't make the bottom row of buttons too low. Find the center of the back with a tape measure and start by positioning the central top button.

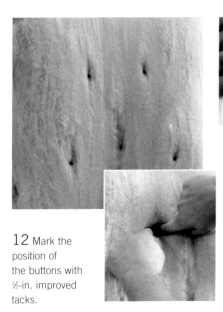

12 Mark the position of the buttons with ½-in. improved tacks.

13(a) When you're happy with your arrangement, you can make the holes. Remove the tacks one at a time and use your fingers to burrow into the layers of stuffing until you reach the scrim. This means that all your buttons will be at the same depth.

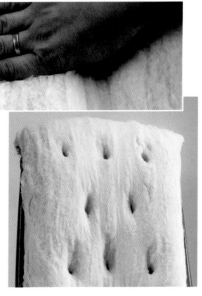

13(b) Stick your thumb in to make sure. Make the other holes in the same way, using your tape measure regularly to insure that the spacing is even.

TOP COVER AND BUTTONING

Measure the top cover and allow an extra 2 in. (5 cm) widthwise and lengthwise for each button. We have three buttons across the width, so added 6 in. (15 cm). For the length, there are three rows of buttons—so again we added 6 in. (15 cm). Remember to allow for the fabric flap at the bottom, which will tuck through under the lower back rail.

14 If you are using an expensive fabric, we recommend that you sew a piece of muslin to the bottom edge of the fabric, where it tucks through to the back and won't be seen. Sew over the seam with another row of stitching to reinforce it. In needlework parlance, this is called "topstitching" and is not to be confused with the upholsterer's term, which means stitching the top roll.

15 Lay the top cover in position but do not tack it on. The button threads act like bridle ties. Starting at the center top button, find the button holes by feeling with your fingers through the top cover. Work the center four buttons first.

16(a) Thread a double-ended straight needle with about 24 in. (60 cm) of 3-ply jute cord. From the front, push the needle right through the pad and then pull it back close to where it first went in.

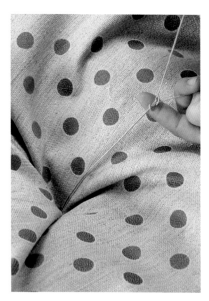

16(b) Make a slip knot (see page 15) so that the two ends of thread are equal in length and hanging from the front. Pull tight. Do the same for all the buttons.

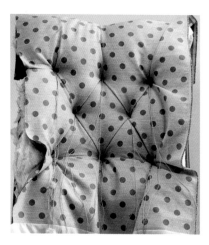

17 As you work, pleats will start to form in the fabric around the holes. Encourage them to pleat with the fold downward, so as not to collect dust, using a wooden pleating tool or the wide end of a regulator. Once you have finished the ties, work on any unruly pleats. Tack the top cover on with ⅜-in. fine tacks inside the show-wood on the sides, and temporary tack onto the top back rail to set the pleats in position.

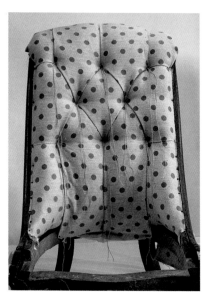

18 Pull the lower edge of the top cover under the lower rail of the outside back and temporary tack it onto the rail.

MAKING AND TYING IN THE BUTTONS

It is usually desirable to make the buttons in the top cover fabric. It is easy to make your own buttons, but a button machine is expensive. A much cheaper option is to have them made by an upholsterer. Most will do this at a negligible cost. We decided to make ours as green dots.

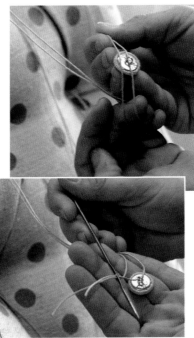

19(a) For each button, thread one of the ties through the button. Then thread both ties through the double-ended straight needle.

19(b) Stick the needle right through to the back.

19(c) Pull tight and tie the ends. Make a little sausage of black-and-white webbing and tie the threads firmly around it.

19(d) This is how the buttoning should look from the front and back.

20 Tidy up the pleats and tack with ⅜-in. fine tacks onto the top back rail.

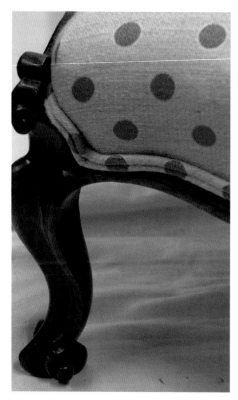

21–37 For the seat, make a sprung stuffed pad in the same way as for the sprung dining chair (page 64) and the gilded chair (page 86), bearing in mind that the fabric at the back will be pulled through between the back and the seat.

Snip into the fabric for the rails, as on the sprung dining chair (page 64) and the gilded chair (page 86).

Sew on a length of muslin (as you did for the back cover) if you wish to conserve your top-cover fabric. This will be pulled through to the back between the seat and the back and tacked onto the lower back rail. The back and side pieces will be concealed by the cover for the outside back panel.

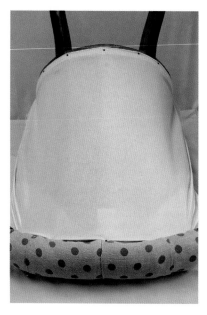

38(a) Measure and cut out muslin to fit across the back and to the start of the show-wood at the front. Folding under, temporary tack the muslin to the lower back rail with ⅜-in. fine tacks.

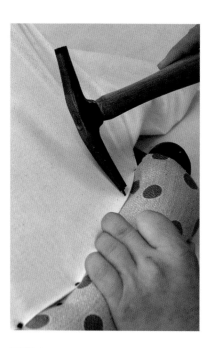

38(b) Temporary tack the muslin to the top back rail to cover the raw edges and the tacking of the inside back cover.

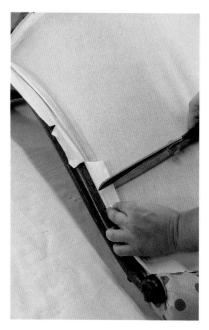

38(c) To allow the fabric to fit neatly around the curved sides, make small cuts as shown. Fold under and temporary tack.

38(d) When you are satisfied with the fit, drive the tacks home.

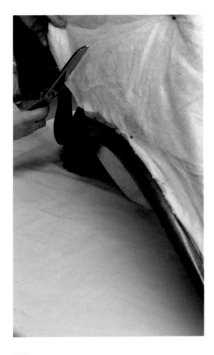

39 Lay two layers of cotton wadding over the muslin and tack sparingly in place.

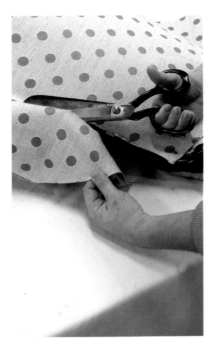

40 Set on your top cover, temporary tacking at top and bottom. Trim off the excess fabric.

41 Slipstitch the top edge (see page 17) and tack down both the sides and the lower edge.

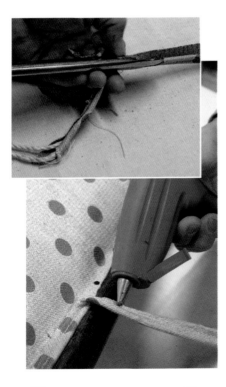

42 Make double piping (see page 19). Glue the double piping into position, in the same way as you would glue a trim.

43 Start at the lower right corner on the back. When it curves out to go around the top of the side rail, secure with a gimp pin.

44 Following the line of the show-wood, trim all around the side rails and across the back. Finish with the bottom cloth (see page 35).

Room screen

This was a pretty, if dog-eared, screen. We felt, however, that the over-blown, fat, pink roses looked rather dated. We decided to keep it looking pretty and rosy, but to give it a more modern slant by pairing a faded-look linen, printed with a simple repeat pattern of roses, on the front of the screen with a clean, pink gingham for the back.

Assuming your screen has three panels, this is a project in which you do the same thing three times. It makes much use of the sewing machine.

TOOLS

Ripping chisel or staple remover
Mallet
Magnetic hammer
Regulator
Tailor's shears
Tape measure
Tailor's chalk
Pins
Sewing machine
Upholsterer's loop pins

MATERIALS

Tacks: ⅜-in. fine
7-oz burlap
Cotton wadding
Top cover
Cotton thread
Six feet (felted glides)
Two piano hinges

ORDER OF WORK

1 Strip (see page 26).

2 Set on the burlap (see page 106).

3 Cut front fabric to size (see page 106).

4 Cut back fabric to size (see page 107).

5 Sew the corners (see page 107).

6 Pin the fabric over the screen (see page 107).

THE ORIGINAL SCREEN
Although the panels themselves were in a good state of repair, the rather overblown floral print and salmon-pink back of the screen looked very dated.

7 Sew the seams (see page 107).

8 Tack cotton wadding onto the frame (see page 108).

9 Slip the cover over the frame (see page 108).

10 Straighten seams with a loop pin (see page 108).

11 Tack fabric onto the bottom (see page 109).

12 Attach the feet (see page 109).

13 Screw on hinges (see page 109).

STRIPPING

1 Having stripped your screen frame, unscrewed the hinges, torn off the old fabric and taken out the tacks and staples, you will end up with three identical simple frames.

SETTING ON THE BURLAP

Lightweight (7-oz) burlap is quite adequate to cover the screen panels, as it is not required to bear any weight.

2(a) Lay out the burlap on the first screen panel and cut to size, allowing an overlap so that you can fold the burlap under. Tension the fabric from side to side, bringing it out from the middle. Do not overstretch the burlap, as this might warp the frame. Temporary tack the corners and hammer in one tack on either side of the frame.

2(b) Tack the corners, holding the burlap taut.

2(c) Tack all around, working from side to side, then from top to bottom. Use the regulator to hold the burlap taut.

CUTTING THE FRONT-COVER FABRIC

We chose roses for the front and gingham for the back of the screen. This brought up the question of where to put the seam. We decided it would be smarter to have the rose material on the sides and the top, so that the seams ran down the back edges. This meant that the front and back fabrics had to be cut to different sizes.

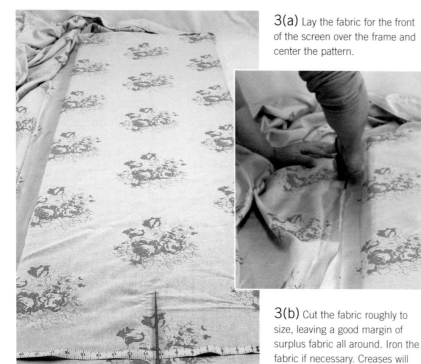

3(a) Lay the fabric for the front of the screen over the frame and center the pattern.

3(b) Cut the fabric roughly to size, leaving a good margin of surplus fabric all around. Iron the fabric if necessary. Creases will show in this project.

3(c) Lay the fabric smoothly over the frame and down the sides, right side up. Using tailor's chalk, draw around the bottom edge of the sides to mark the stitching line, then draw another line ⅜ in. (1 cm) away to mark the cutting line. If there is a shape at the top of the screen, as there is in ours, be sure to cut around it.

CUTTING THE BACK-COVER FABRIC

Because the seam line between the front and back fabrics will be positioned level with the back of the panel, you do not need to add on the measurement for the sides of the frame when you cut out the back fabric. Simply add on a ⅜-in. (1-cm) seam allowance.

4 Measure and cut the fabric for the back of the frame, adding on a ⅜-in. (1-cm) seam allowance as for the front.

SEWING THE CORNERS

These are tiny seams, but worth taking care over as they will anchor the cover neatly in position for the next steps.

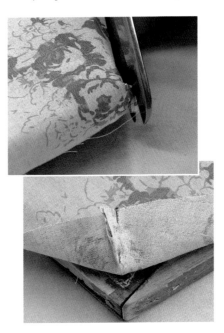

5(a) Place the front fabric on the screen right side up to check the pattern, then pin. Then repin on the wrong side and trim the corners.

5(b) Machine stitch the corners on the wrong side and trim the seam allowance.

PINNING THE FABRIC OVER THE SCREEN

It's important to pin the fabric cover over the screen before you stitch the front and back together, so that you can check the fit, ensuring that the two corners meet.

6 Place the fabric for the front of the screen on your work surface, right side up, then center the screen panel on top. Lay the fabric for the back of the screen on top, right side down. In the center of each long side of each fabric, cut a notch almost up to the seam line. Working from this point outward on each side, pin the two fabrics together along the side and top edges, ensuring the corners meet.

SEWING THE SEAMS

Because the fabric needs to fit snugly, we measured a ⅜-in. (1-cm) seam allowance in Steps 3(c) and 4, but worked to a ½-in. (1.25-cm) seam when stitching. This allows for the stretch of the fabric, but also means that your measurements must be absolutely accurate.

7 Machine stitch along the side and top, taking a ½-in. (1.25-cm) seam and removing the pins as you go.

TACKING ON THE COTTON WADDING

Only a single layer of cotton wadding is needed for this project. It works to soften the edges, both visually and in terms of protecting the top cover from rubbing on the wooden frame. You are not going to sit on it, however, so comfort is not an issue.

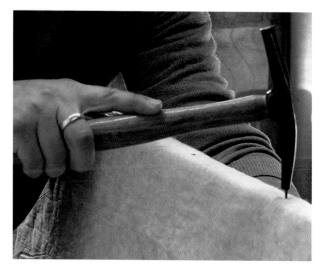

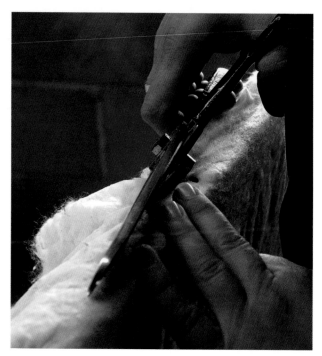

8(a) Cut a layer of cotton wadding to fit both sides. Using ⅜-in. fine tacks, tack it in place along the side edges of the panel. Make sure it is secure so that it stays in position when you pull on the top cover.

8(b) Trim off any excess cotton wadding.

FITTING THE COVER AND ASSEMBLING THE SCREEN

The cover will be a tight fit and you will probably have to do a lot of pulling and maneuvering to fit it onto the panel, but take your time.

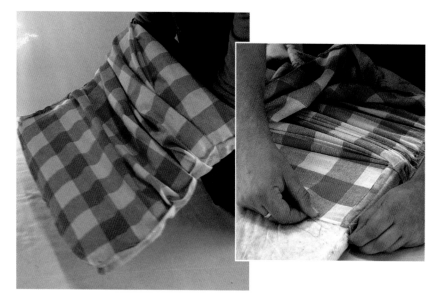

9 Turn the cover right side out and then slip it over the frame. It is important to keep the seams straight.

10 Once the cover is on, use a loop pin to straighten out any kinks or folds in the seams, so that they align perfectly with the back edge of the panel.

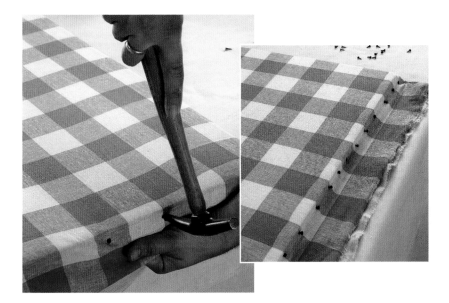

11(a) Tack the back fabric along the bottom edge of the panel and cut off any excess. Fold the raw edge of the front fabric under, so that the fold aligns with the bottom edge of the back of the panel, and tack in place. Trim the overlap and, in the same way, tack the front cover over, turning the edge under to form a neat, folded edge.

11(b) Iron lightly to set the fabric smoothly.

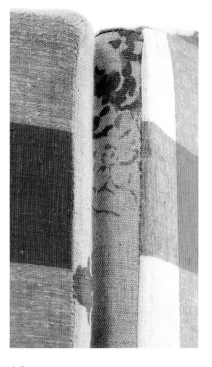

12 Fix small feet to the bottom of the screen.

13 Now, carry out the same process with the other two frames. When all are finished, screw on the hinges. We used long piano hinges so that only one hinge is needed between each pair of panels.

Edwardian recliner

This Edwardian reclining chair was in a sorry state of repair, but we felt there was something rather fun about it. It has a simple sliding mechanism under the seat, allowing you to sprawl.

The chair has a modern simplicity to it and a cheerful, contemporary fabric was called for; we chose stylized flowers and circles in bright green and turquoise. We also used tinted wax to make the wood a warm, deep brown.

This project demonstrates how to use fabric in a back panel and how to upholster a spring unit. It also introduces decorative nailing.

TOOLS

Ripping chisel or staple remover
Mallet
Magnetic hammer
Tailor's shears
Tape measure
Tailor's chalk
5-in. 15-gauge curved needle
Double-ended straight needle
Sewing machine
Upholsterer's loop pins

MATERIALS

Tacks: ½-in. improved, ⅜-in. improved, ⅜-in. fine
3-ply jute cord
10-oz burlap
Horsehair
Linen scrim
Muslin
Cotton wadding and felt
Piping cord
Top cover
Decorative nails
Bottom cloth

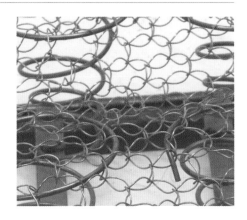

THE ORIGINAL CHAIR
At first glance, this reclining chair looked to be irreparably damaged. However, the frame was solid and only required rewaxing while the spring unit in the seat was in good order, so we were able to reuse it.

STRIPPING

1 Strip the chair and remove the back. At this point we waxed the wood with tinted wax to bring out the color.

ORDER OF WORK

1 Strip (see page 26).

BACK

2 Fix the top-cover fabric to the outside back of the chair (see below).

3 Lay on the cotton wadding and burlap (see page 113).

4 Make the stuffing ties and stuff with a shallow layer of horsehair (see pages 30–31 and 113).

5 Measure, cut out and set on the muslin (see page 113).

6 Lay on a second layer of cotton wadding (see page 114).

7 Measure, cut out and set on the top cover (see page 114).

8 Neaten the corners (see page 114).

9 Finish with decorative nailing (see page 114).

SEAT

10 Attach the spring unit to the wooden base (see page 115).

11 Set on the burlap (see page 115).

12 Tuck in the corners of the burlap and blanket stitch in place (see page 115).

13 Attach the burlap to the top wire of the spring unit using blanket stitch (see page 115).

14 Make the bridle and stuffing ties (see pages 42 and 30).

15 Stuff with horsehair (see page 31).

16 Set on the scrim with loop pins (see pages 116).

17 Make the bridle ties (see page 42).

18 Neaten the corners (see page 116).

19 Regulate the stuffing and topstitch the scrim to the spring unit (see pages 43 and 46).

20 Sew the muslin cap (see page 117).

21 Check the muslin cap on the pad for size (see page 118).

22 Use the muslin cap as a template for cutting out the top cover (see page 118).

23 Make a stuffing of cotton wadding (see page 119).

24 Tack on the muslin cap (see page 119).

25 Make the piping, sew the piping to the top of the top cover and sew on the side panels (see pages 18 and 119).

26 Set on the top cover, finish with decorative nailing, finish with the bottom cloth, and reassemble the chair (see page 119).

OUTSIDE BACK   FIXING THE TOP COVER

The padded back of the chair is built up in layers, starting with the back of the top cover. Make sure that the right side of the fabric faces outward and leave a good margin of tack wood to fix subsequent layers.

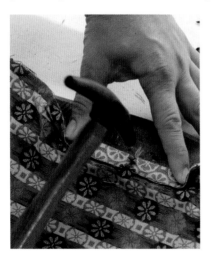

2(a) Cut the back of the top cover to fit the frame (see page 33). Working from the inside of the frame and using ⅜-in. improved tacks, temporary tack the fabric at the top, folding the edges in.

2(b) Temporary tack the fabric at the bottom of the frame. Keep turning the frame over as you work to check that the fabric is lying square and smooth. Make sure that the pattern is in line with the show-wood. When you are satisfied, knock the tacks in.

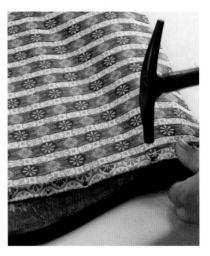

2(c) The fabric must lie smoothly in the curve of the frame. Keep the tension from top to bottom. Tack the sides, then fold the raw edges up and over, keeping them in place with tacks spaced 3 in. (7.5 cm) apart. These edges will be concealed by subsequent layers. Trim off any surplus fabric.

LAYING ON COTTON WADDING AND BURLAP

Remember that you are working backward at this point, so the cotton wadding comes before the burlap.

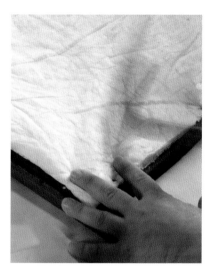

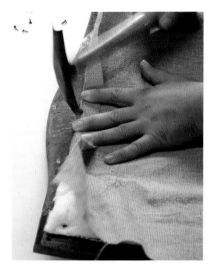

3(a) Cut a double layer of cotton wadding to size. Tack the cotton wadding in position, using ⅜-in. fine tacks. Trim the edges.

3(b) Cut 10-oz burlap to size. Tack it on in the same way as the back of the top cover, making sure that the tension is from top to bottom and that the burlap lies smoothly.

MAKING THE STUFFING TIES AND STUFFING WITH HORSEHAIR

Make only a shallow stuffing, as this is a flat-backed chair.

4 Using a curved needle and 3-ply jute cord, make the stuffing ties (see page 30). Work a square 2 in. (5 cm) inside the tack line, then make a line down the middle, making sure you don't stitch through the top cover. Stuff with horsehair.

SETTING ON THE MUSLIN

Be prepared for it to be quite hard work to pull the muslin over the horsehair.

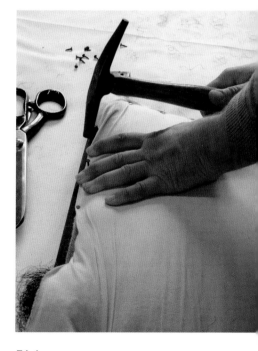

5(a) Cut the muslin to size and lay it over the frame. We followed the chair's original covering and brought the muslin up onto the top of the frame. Temporary tack the muslin at the bottom, then pull to the top.

5(b) As you tack the sides and bottom of the frame, roll the horsehair under to clear the show-wood, then tuck the muslin under and tack along the fold line about ¼ in. (0.5 cm) from the edge to allow space for the top cover and the decorative nailing.

5(c) As you tack the sides, be sure not to pull the muslin too tight, so you maintain the curve of the back.

COTTON WADDING

6 We used a second double layer of cotton wadding over the muslin to add volume and cushioning. We had considered using cotton felt, but felt this would be too bulky and would put too much pressure on the rails. Lay the cotton wadding on, smoothing it into the curve of the back. Tack it sparingly into position.

SETTING ON THE TOP COVER

Once you have measured and cut out the front of the top cover, notch the center of each side. Mark the center point of each side of the frame with tailor's chalk. Lay the fabric over, aligning the marks on the fabric and frame. Temporary tack from top to bottom and from side to side.

7 Tack only every 2 in. (5 cm), as you will remove the tacks when you knock in the decorative nailing that will hold the top cover in position.

8 Fold over the corners neatly. If you wish, you can hold them in position with the pointed end of the regulator.

9(a) Use a magnetic hammer to knock in the decorative nails, keeping them close together to form an unbroken line. Start in one corner and work around the panel.

9(b) Remove the tacks as you work.

9(c) Hammer carefully so you don't damage the domed head of the nail.

SEAT ATTACHING THE SPRING UNIT

A spring unit does the same job as springs. Ours was in good condition and we were able to reuse it. If you have one that is broken, you may find it easier to resort to conventional springs and webbing, because spring units are difficult to repair. You will often find such spring units on Victorian beds and Edwardian chairs.

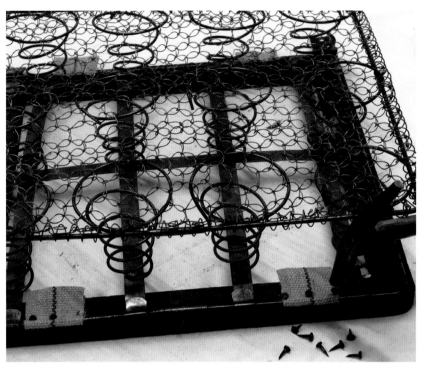

10 Fix the spring unit onto the wooden base. At each end of the spring unit, fold two short lengths of jute or black-and-white webbing over the base wire and secure onto the wooden base with three ½-in. improved tacks. You need to use large tacks, as they have to hold the spring unit in position.

SETTING ON THE BURLAP

11 Cut the burlap so that it's large enough to pull down over the spring unit and secure it to the wooden base with ⅜-in. improved tacks, folding under the raw edges. Leave a margin for the top cover and the decorative nailing.

12 Tuck the corners in and pin them in place. Using a curved needle and 3-ply jute cord, blanket stitch the corners (see page 17).

13 Blanket stitch the burlap to the top edge, looping the needle under the wire of the spring unit. This is important for bonding the burlap to the spring unit.

MAKING THE BRIDLE AND STUFFING TIES

The bridle ties hold the burlap to the springs. The stuffing ties are looser to allow stuffing with horsehair.

14 Make bridle ties (see page 42) along three sides, then up through the middle. As you work, hook the top wire layer with the needle. This will prevent the burlap from slipping around on top of the springs. Make stuffing ties (see page 30) in the shape of one square inside another.

STUFFING WITH HORSEHAIR

15 Make a dense, even stuffing of horsehair.

SETTING ON THE SCRIM AND MAKING BRIDLE TIES

16 Cut the scrim to come down over the horsehair. Tuck the edges under the horsehair, then pull down the folded edge and pin it into position on the burlap.

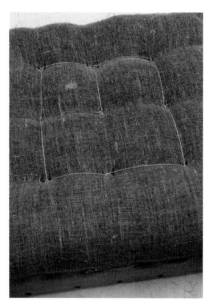

17 Make bridle ties (see page 42) in the shape of a square, with two stitches to each side and two stitches up the middle. Be careful not to get the cord entangled in the springs.

NEATENING THE CORNERS

18 Tuck in the corners neatly and secure with loop pins.

TOPSTITCHING

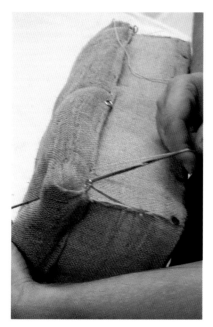

19(a) Regulate the stuffing into the corners. Topstitch under the top edge wire of the spring unit to make a top-roll and secure the scrim. This one row of stitching is enough to achieve all these steps.

19(b) Remove the loop pins as you work and keep regulating the stuffing to the front.

19(c) You will end up with a pad that looks like this.

SEWING THE MUSLIN CAP

You now need to make a cap of muslin—in effect, half a box cushion. This uses a sewing machine. Be sure to measure accurately, as the cap will serve as a template for the top cover.

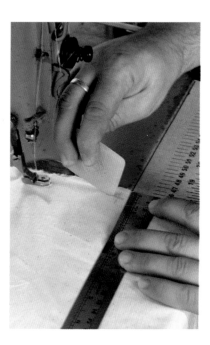

20(a) Measure the top of the pad, allowing an extra ¾ in. (2 cm) all around for the seam allowance, and cut out in muslin. Measure the depth and the length of all four sides, adding an extra ½ in. (1.25 cm) to the length for the seams, and cut out.

20(b) Machine stitch the side panel to the top panel, with the side panel uppermost. Mark the corner with tailor's chalk.

20(c) Make one chalk mark ½ in. (1.25 cm) back from the corner mark, for the seam allowance. Make another mark ½ in. (1.25 cm) from the seam that you're sewing. This will make a cross.

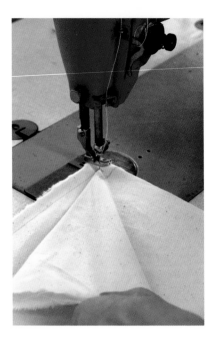

20(d) Snip across the width of the seam, level with the intersection of the cross.

20(e) Continue sewing until you reach the chalked cross. With the needle down, holding the fabric, lift up the sewing machine foot.

20(f) Turn the corner, folding the side panel back at a right angle. Continue sewing around the square.

CHECKING THE MUSLIN CAP FOR SIZE

If the muslin cap fits well, use it as a template for cutting out the top cover. If not, adjust the seams.

CUTTING THE TOP COVER

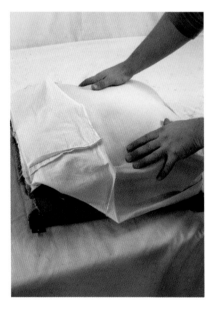

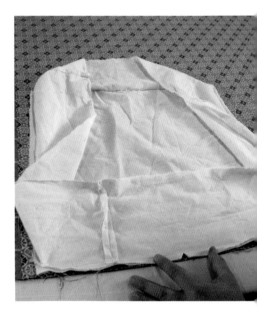

21(a) Check the fit by setting on the muslin cap on the pad right side up and pulling up the sides to reveal the seam. This will show whether or not the seams align with the top edges of the pad. Adjust if necessary.

21(b) Loop pin the muslin to the pad through the seam to check there is no looseness.

22 If you are satisfied that the muslin cap fits well, remove the loop pins and use the cap as a template to cut out the top cover.

LAYING ON COTTON FELT AND TACKING ON MUSLIN CAP

23 Lay on cotton felt over the border edges to pack out the sides.

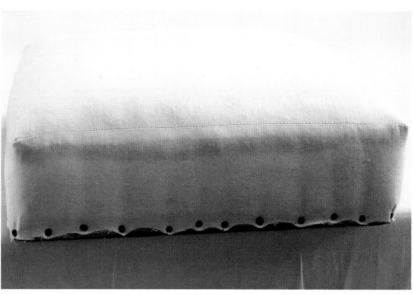

24 Reposition the muslin on the pad and tack it onto the wooden base, leaving a margin for setting on the top cover with decorative nailing. To avoid bulk, we did not fold under the muslin but trimmed it just below the tacks. Apply a double layer of cotton wadding before fitting the cover.

MAKING PIPING AND SETTING ON THE TOP COVER

The top cover is sewn in much the same way as the muslin layer, with the addition of piping. Start by measuring around the top of the pad and making a length of piping (see page 18).

25 Place the top panel right side up and lay on the piping, aligning the raw edges so that the corded side of the piping faces inward. Machine stitch, stitching as close to the piping cord as possible. Machine stitch the side panel onto the top panel, as you did with the muslin. Check the fit.

26 Fix the top cover with temporary tacks and decorative nailing, carefully turning under the raw edges, just as you did for the back. Tack on the bottom cloth (see page 35) and reassemble the chair.

Box cushion

Church pews and benches have become very popular. The narrow seats with storage space underneath make them an attractive option in halls and kitchens where space is tight. Yet there's no arguing with the discomfort of sitting on a pew for any length of time—undoubtedly a design feature to stop you from nodding off during long sermons.

We looked for a way of softening the experience of sitting on our 18th-century Welsh pew without detracting from its appealing austerity. Feather cushions would be too bulky and would slide around. We opted instead to make a simple box cushion using reconstituted foam, which is recycled.

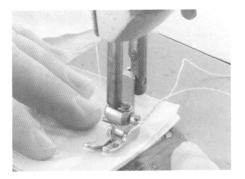

TOOLS

Tailor's shears
Tape measure
Pins
Sewing machine
Small curved needle

MATERIALS

Reconstituted foam
Cotton wadding
Spray contact adhesive
Top cover
Cotton thread

ORDER OF WORK

1 Measure the seat and get the foam cut to size. (Your supplier will do this.)

2 Stick two layers of cotton wadding to the top and sides of the pad (see page 122).

3 Measure and cut out the side panels and the top and bottom pieces (see page 122).

4 Machine stitch the side panels together and topstitch the seams (see page 122).

5 Machine stitch the side panel to the top and bottom panels, leaving the back seam open (see page 123).

6 Slipstitch the back seam (see page 123).

RECONSTITUTED FOAM PAD

Reconstituted foam provides a large amount of support even when thin. We used foam that is 2 in. (5 cm) deep.

1 Get your supplier to cut the foam to the size you want.

COTTON WADDING

Cotton wadding provides extra softness and softens any hard edges.

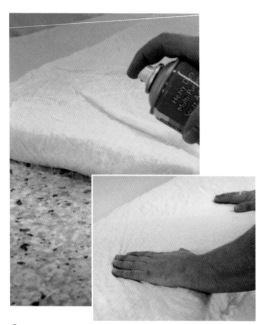

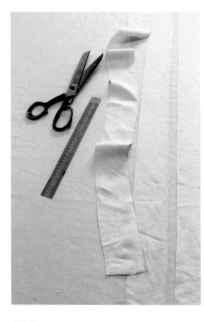

2 Using spray contact adhesive, stick two layers of cotton wadding onto the top and sides of the pad, furry side down. Smooth out the cotton wadding with your hands. The adhesive will dry in seconds.

CUTTING OUT THE CUSHION COVER

If you are recycling old fabric, as we did, make sure you choose areas that are not worn. We decided to use the embroidered initials in the top right corner, adding a very pretty detail on an essentially plain cover.

3(a) Measure the top, bottom and sides, allowing an extra ½ in. (1.25 cm) all around for the seams.

3(b) Cut a sliver off both angles of the corners. This softens the sewn corners and prevents those little "ears" that you see sometimes.

SEWING THE CUSHION COVER

We used topstitch for all the seams, which adds a decorative detail and makes the seams more able to withstand wear. The needlework term "topstitch" should not be confused with the upholsterer's term. In this context, it means machine stitching over the seams.

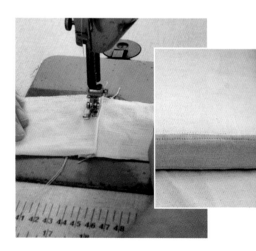

3(c) Cut out the side panels in two pieces. Cut one long piece to go around the front and sides, plus 4 in. (10 cm) on each side to run around onto the back. Cut out one back piece that is the length of the back minus the 4 in. (10 cm) on each end.

4(a) With right sides together, taking ½-in. (1.25-cm) seams, machine stitch the side pieces together. Press open the seams.

4(b) Turn the fabric right side up and, using the foot as a guide, machine stitch over the seam. Inset: This is what topstitching means in sewing terms.

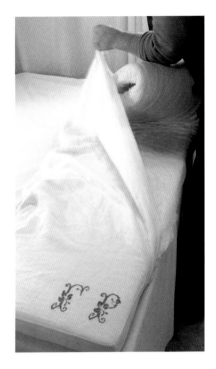

5(a) With right sides together, pin the side panel to the top panel.

5(b) Machine stitch, removing the pins as you go. Now pin and machine stitch the top part of the cushion to the bottom panel, leaving the back seam open. Topstitch all the seams. Snip off any excess fabric at the corners to reduce bulk.

5(c) Turn the cushion cover right side out and iron if necessary. Insert the foam pad into the cover.

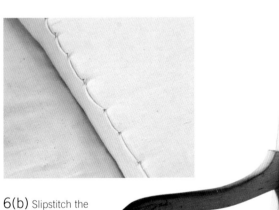

6(b) Slipstitch the bottom back seam by hand, removing the pins as you work. We decided not to use a zip, as the effect would be too bulky. The seam can easily be unpicked for washing and can quickly be restitched.

6(a) Fold under the raw edges of the fabric along the bottom back seam and pin the fabrics together.

Day bed

Soft white paint and a modern chintz transformed this dreary day bed. The old red velour conjured up images of gloomy afternoons dragging, to the sound of clocks slowly ticking. In its new guise there would be birds singing, the warm scent of roses, and idle but amusing chat.

This project shows you how to recover a day bed, in which the existing upholstery is sound. We need to define our terms. The upholstered and painted upright is the "back panel." The rounded top of the arm is the "top roll." The "scroll arm" is the curved end of the day bed.

TOOLS

Ripping chisel or staple remover
Mallet
Tailor's shears
Tape measure and tailor's chalk
Sewing machine
Magnetic hammer and pins
Wooden pleating tool or regulator
Small curved needle
Webbing stretcher
5-in. 15-gauge curved needle
Upholsterer's loop pins
Hot glue gun and glue sticks

MATERIALS

Cotton wadding
Top cover
Tacks: ⅜-in. improved, ⅜-in. fine
Gimp pins
Cotton thread
Piping cord for thin fabric
Waxed slipping thread
10-oz burlap
3-ply jute cord
Horsehair
Muslin
Braid

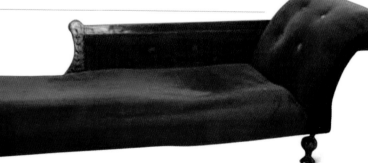

THE ORIGINAL DAY BED
The bed was covered in a shabby, dark-red velour that looked heavy and depressingly uninviting—certainly not a luxurious piece of furniture on which to lounge.

ORDER OF WORK

1 Unscrew the back panel and remove the existing fabric and cotton wadding, leaving the muslin intact. Rub down and paint the woodwork (see page 126).

2 Decide on the pattern placing (see page 126).

ARM

3 Measure and cut the arm top-cover fabric (see page 127).

4 Sew a length of muslin onto the top cover to tuck through to the back (see page 127).

5 Tack on two layers of cotton wadding and set on the top cover (see page 127).

6 Cut the fabric to fit around the rails (see page 127).

7 Tuck the bottom edge through to the back, then fold under and tack the side pieces (see page 127).

8 Make pleats around the top roll (see page 128).

9 Adjust the tacks, then trim off excess fabric (see page 128).

10 Make piping for the scroll (see page 18) and tack in place (see page 129).

11 Fit cotton wadding inside the piping (see page 129).

12 Fit the top cover inside the piping (see page 129).

13 Slipstitch in place (see page 17).

14 Work the back scroll in a similar way, but only down to the top of the back rail (see page 129).

SEAT

15 Decide on the pattern placement.

16 Cut out and position the fabric.

17 Lay on two layers of cotton wadding.

18 Set on the top cover.

19 Cut out the border, matching up the pattern.

20 Make piping (see page 18).

21 Sew the piping to the border (see page 119).

22 Pin the piped border around the seat.

23 Slipstitch the border into position (see page 17).

24 Tack the lower edge of the border under the frame.

BACK PANEL
INSIDE BACK PANEL

25 Strip to the frame if necessary (see page 26).

26 Position and fix the webbing (see page 26).

27 Fix the burlap base (see page 28).

28 Make stuffing ties (see page 30).

29 Stuff with horsehair (see page 31).

30 Set on the muslin (see page 32).

31 Lay on cotton wadding (see page 32).

32 Set on the top cover (see page 33).

33 Attach the trim (see page 38).

34 Screw the back panel into position.

OUTSIDE BACK PANEL

35 Tack on the muslin (see pages 32 and 92).

36 Lay on two layers of cotton wadding (see pages 32 and 92).

37 Set on the top cover (see pages 33 and 92).

38 Tack the lower edge under the frame.

39 Attach the trimming (see page 38).

OUTSIDE ARM

40 Tack on the muslin (see pages 32 and 92).

41 Lay on two layers of cotton wadding (see pages 32 and 92).

42 Set on the top cover, tacking with gimp pins (see pages 92 and 129).

43 Tack the lower edge under the frame.

44 Finish with bottom cloth (see page 35).

STRIPPING AND PREPARING THE FRAME

We hesitate to use such a violent term as "stripping" here. You need to work carefully, gently removing tacks so that you don't damage the pads or tear the muslin. The upholstery on the back panel of our day bed, however, was very tatty so we stripped it down to the frame and started from scratch.

1 Unscrew and remove the back panel. Strip the day bed down to the muslin, taking off the top cover and cotton wadding. Rub down the show-wood and paint it in your chosen color.

PLACING THE PATTERN

There is a strong element of pattern-matching in this project as well as piping, both of which demand extra fabric. If you choose a large pattern, as we did, take advice on the length of pattern repeat. You will need to order extra fabric and there will be some wastage.

2(a) Lay the fabric over the day bed and decide how to place the pattern. Our chosen fabric was a composition of birds and roses. As the day bed is more likely to be looked at from the side than from the end, we decided to run the pattern across the seat rather than down the length. We intended to use green braid on the back panel, so we concentrated the rose motif, with its green leaves, on the seat to pick up the color.

2(b) The blue parrots were delightful on the arm. Even in an asymmetric pattern such as this, it is important to decide on a central point. Although the corbel seemed an obvious choice, we felt the tail of the bird on the left unbalanced the composition and chose instead the perch of the smallest bird in the middle. Use a tape measure to establish the center. Measure the width (remembering to keep your central point), allowing for enough fabric to pleat around the scrolls (curved sides).

ARM COTTON WADDING, SETTING ON THE TOP COVER

Keep checking with your tape measure as you work, to insure that the pattern is centered.

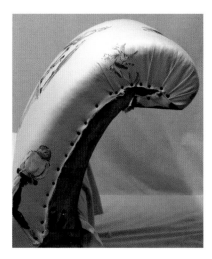

3 Measure the length of the arm from the back underside of the top roll, allowing enough fabric to pull through between the back and the seat, and tack it in place using ⅜-in. fine tacks. It is advisable to lay the fabric on the piece and check before you cut it out. If you are using expensive fabric, follow the tip in the next step.

4 Machine stitch a piece of muslin to the lower edge of the panel to tuck through under the arm. This saves you from wasting expensive material.

5(a) Fix two layers of cotton wadding onto the arm, tacking them in place with ⅜-in. fine tacks, and then set on the top cover. Temporary tack the top cover into position on the scrolls and the outside top rail at the back of the arm, making sure that the pattern is centered.

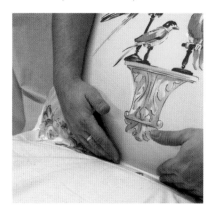

5(b) Smooth the fabric along the crease between the base of the arm and the seat, to insure that the muslin will be concealed.

6(a) On both sides, make a Y-cut (see page 135) up to the crease, as shown.

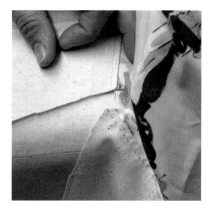

6(b) Notch the fabric, as shown, on both sides. This will allow the fabric to go around the side rail.

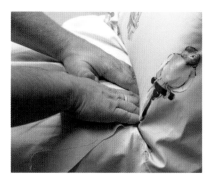

6(c) Push the muslin flap through the gap under the arm.

7 Go to the back and pull the flap through and tack it onto the lower outside rail. Pull down the side pieces, then fold the edges under and tack them taut, using ⅜-in. fine tacks.

PLEATING THE SCROLL AT THE SIDE OF THE TOP ROLL

There will be looseness around the edge of the top roll, which allows you to pleat the fabric. The pleats should be evenly spaced.

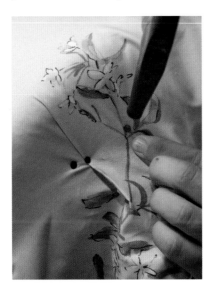

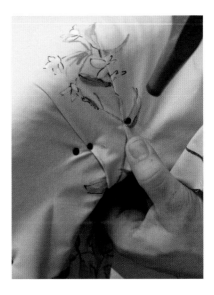

8(a) Make sure your hands are scrupulously clean so that you don't mark the fabric as you pleat. Temporary tack the fabric to the top roll so that it lies snugly on the scroll. Knock in a tack to hold the fabric.

8(b) Make a neat, sharp pleat, creasing the fabric with your fingers, and pull the pleat over the tack.

8(c) Tack to hold.

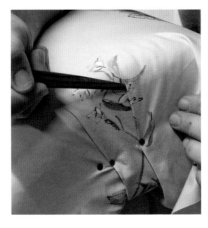

8(d) Using a wooden pleating tool or the wide end of a regulator, smooth up under the pleat and take out any fullness. Stop pleating where the top rail starts to curve in toward the back.

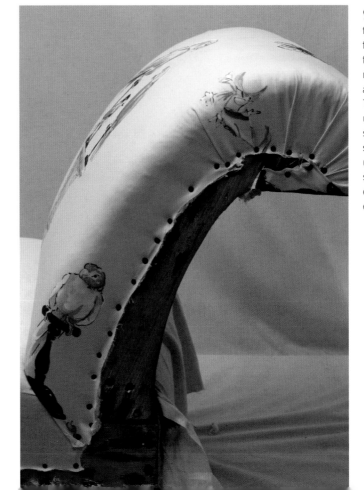

9 Adjust the tacks holding the fabric on the outside top rail to take out any looseness. Tack the sides up onto the scroll, as shown. Tack up the scroll as shown, then cut off the excess fabric.

ADDING PIPING AROUND THE SCROLL

The twist of standard piping would have been visible through our thin fabric, so we used narrow woven piping.

10 Tack on piping around the scroll, starting at the seat and curving around the scroll and down the back corner to the base of the frame. As you reach the outside top panel, snip into the raw edges of the piping so that you can twist it to start tacking it onto the back of the frame.

11 Fit two layers of cotton wadding into the area enclosed by the piping and tack, using ⅜-in. fine tacks.

12 Choose your pattern for the scroll facing. We chose roses to pick up the roses on the seat. The fabric needs to reach down just below the bottom of the arm, where the edge will be covered by the border. Cut the facing to shape. Fold under the raw edges and pin in position so that the edge of the facing hides the raw edges and joins neatly with the piping.

BACK SCROLL

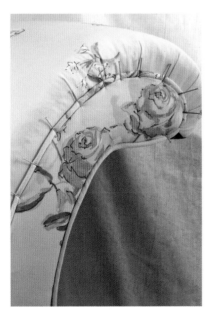

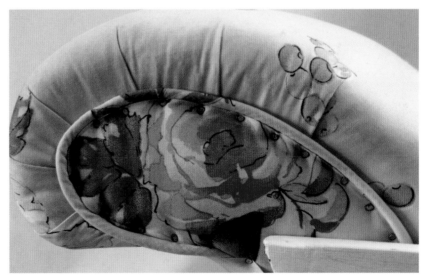

13 Using a curved needle and waxed slipping thread, slipstitch the facing into place.

14 Only the top of the scroll is visible when the back panel is in position, so only this part needs to be worked. On this side, we used gimp pins to fix the scroll panel rather than slipstitch. You may choose whichever method you prefer.

SEAT

15–24 The seat is covered in the same way as the long footstool (see page 58), although we worked the piped border differently. Refer to the Order of Work on page 124, but note the following points:

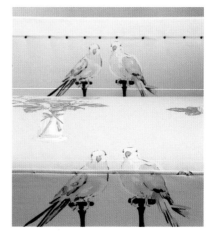

• Set on the top cover in the same way as for the long footstool (see page 60). Leave a length of fabric at the arm end to push through to the back or sew on a length of muslin, as we did for the arm panel.

• The border around the sides runs to the back of the arm across the front facing, covering the lower section of the scroll. At the back, it stops at the point where the back panel is attached.

• Sew the piping onto the border in the same way as for the Edwardian recliner (see page 119).

• Pin the piping in place, using a sliding bevel or ruler to keep it straight.

• Slipstitch the piping to the seat, working your stitches behind the top edge of the piping so they are hidden.

• Tack the lower edge of the border under the frame.

Skilful pattern-matching turns a pretty day bed into a fabulous day bed. It is definitely worth the expense of fabric. Here you can see how we recreated the pair of birds with the border and echoed the pattern on the back panel.

BACK PANEL INSIDE BACK PANEL

25–34 We stripped the back panel and entirely reupholstered the frame. Upholster the inside of the back panel before you screw it back into place, in the same way as for the pin-stuffed chair (see page 36). Braid should be fixed on the lefthand vertical and across the top; elsewhere, all the tacks will be hidden by the seat and the arm.

OUTSIDE BACK PANEL

35–39 Screw the back panel into position before you cover the outside, as the cover will hide the fixings. Cover it in the same way as for the back of the gilded chair (see page 92). Tack the lower edge of the fabric under the frame and attach braid on two sides, as shown.

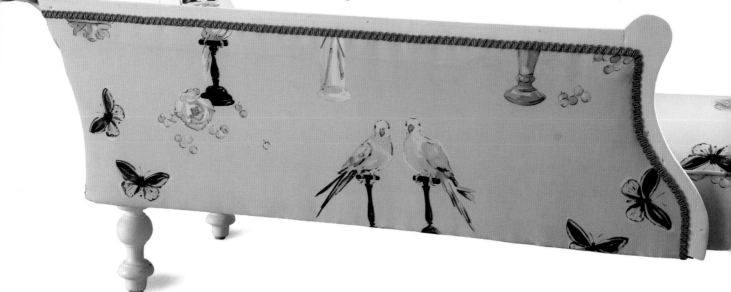

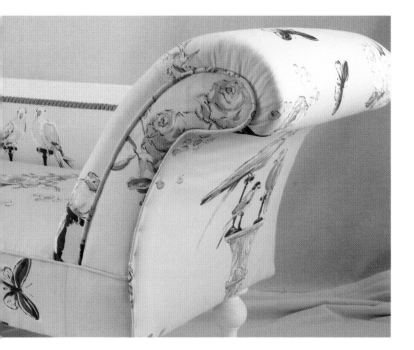

OUTSIDE OF ARM

40–43 We repeated the motif of blue parrots on the outside of the arm. Cover it in the same way as you did the outside of the back panel. Then either slipstitch it into position or tack it with gimp pins, as we did. Keep your tension from side to side so that you maintain the curve of the back of the arm. Tack the lower edge of the fabric under the frame.

FINISH WITH BOTTOM CLOTH

44 For such a light fabric, we recommend using muslin for the bottom cloth.

Stripped of its oppressive, dark-red, dust-filled velour and with a coat of soft white paint and a light, modern chintz, the day bed was transformed.

Tub chair

Like the day bed (page 124), this armchair is a recovering project. You will need to use a sewing machine to fit the covers around the curved back and arms. We chose a silver-green fabric with an Edwardian feel to recover this tub chair. Closer inspection reveals a pattern of Lowryesque dancing people—a modern twist on the traditional sprig. In tackling such a project for the first time, you would be well advised to choose a fabric that does not call for complicated pattern matching.

This project requires piping and slipstitching skills. The scrolls are worked in the same way as the day bed arms. Temporary tacking to stretch the fabric to a perfect fit is essential here.

TOOLS	MATERIALS
Ripping chisel or staple remover	Top cover
Mallet	Cotton felt
Tape measure and tailor's chalk	Cotton wadding
Tailor's shears	Tacks: ⅜-in. fine
Sewing machine	Italian hemp twine
Magnetic hammer and pins	Piping cord
Wooden pleating tool or	
wide end of regulator	

THE ORIGINAL CHAIR
This worn old tub chair had kept its figure but desperately needed a smart new cover. We kept the Edwardian mood and added two rows of piping at the back.

SEAT MEASURING FOR THE TOP COVER

There is no feather cushion on this armchair, so the sprung stuff-over seat pad is softened with a layer of cotton felt.

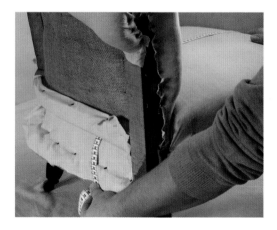

2 Measure for the top cover. Push the tape measure between the lower rail of the arms and the bottom rail. For the width, measure from the lower edge of the bottom rail, over the seat, and down to the lower edge on the other side, and then add 4 in. (10 cm). For the length, measure from the bottom of the front rail, over the seat and through the back, down to the lower edge of the bottom rail and add 4 in. (10 cm).

ORDER OF WORK

1 Strip to the muslin (see page 26).

SEAT

2 Measure for the top cover (see page 134).

3 Cut out the top cover and notch the center of each side (see page 134).

4 Lay cotton felt on the seat (see page 135).

5 Lay on cotton wadding (see page 135).

6 Measure the center on each side of the base of the pad, mark with tailor's chalk and set on the top cover (see page 135).

7 Make cuts to front and back to fit the fabric around the uprights and pull the fabric through to the outside (see page 135).

8 Tack onto the outside bottom rail on the sides and back (see page 136).

9 Tack at the front, pleating the corners to fit (see page 136).

10 Trim any surplus fabric (see page 137).

BACK AND ARMS

11 Establish the positioning of the seams using Italian hemp twine (see page 137).

12 Measure and cut two arm pieces and one for the back (see page 137).

13 Lay the arm pieces into position and fold over at the seam lines. Make cuts in the overlap to make the fabric flexible (see page 138).

14 Lay on the back piece and treat in the same way. Pin the seams in place (see page 138).

15 Trim the seams (see page 138).

16 Remove the fabric (see page 139).

17 Make single piping (see page 18). Sew on the piping (see page 139).

18 Sew arm and back pieces together (see page 139).

19 Lay on the cotton felt (see page 140).

20 Tack on the cotton wadding (see page 140).

21 Fit on the top cover and temporary tack at top back. Fit the fabric around the uprights, tucking down and pulling through (see page 140).

22 Tack on the arm sections. Tack the pulled-through fabric onto the bottom rail at the sides and back (see page 140).

SCROLLS, FRONT BORDER AND PIPING

23 Tuck and pleat the fabric around the scroll (see pages 128 and 141).

24 Trim any surplus fabric (see page 141).

25 Make the piped front border (see page 18). Slipstitch and tack the border in place (see pages 130 and 142).

26 Trim the surplus fabric from the pulled-through flaps and tack over (see page 142).

OUTSIDE BACK AND ARM PANELS

27 Pipe the scroll, pad with cotton wadding and slipstitch the scroll facing (see page 142).

28 Measure and cut out two outside arm panels and one back panel. Tack and slipstitch the arm panels in place (see pages 102 and 143).

29 Finish with the bottom cloth (see page 35).

CUTTING OUT THE TOP COVER

3(a) Cut the top cover to these measurements. With such a tiny pattern find a central line and work out from that. This fabric has a pattern of tiny dancing people so it is important that they should not be standing on their heads; there is a right way up.

3(b) Notch the center of each side of the fabric to insure correct positioning. The easiest way to do this is to fold the fabric in half and snip off a tiny corner at each end of the fold. Then fold the other way and snip again. You will now have central notches in all four sides of your fabric.

LAYING ON COTTON FELT AND COTTON WADDING

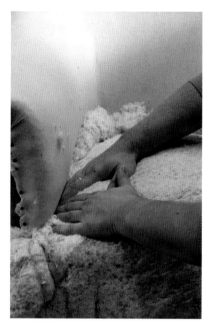

4(a) Lay on the cotton felt, tearing it to size, bearing in mind that the edges will be pushed down into the side of the seat pad.

4(b) Push the edges of the felt down the sides and back of the seat. You can see in the picture that not much overlap is needed. Tear off at the front so it just sits over the edge of the seat.

5 Set on a folded double layer of cotton wadding. Again, not much overlap is needed to push down the sides and back of the seat. Leave some overlap at the front sides. Trim as shown.

SETTING ON THE TOP COVER

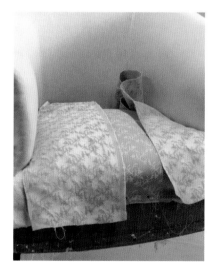

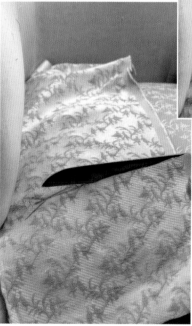

6 Measure the center of all four sides of the base of the seat pad and mark with tailor's chalk. Lay on the fabric, aligning the central notches with the chalk marks. Knock in three or four tacks to hold the fabric on the center of the front rail, leaving 5 in. (12.5 cm) untacked at each end. Fold the overlap on each side inward so that the fold just tucks down the side.

7(a) In line with the front of the arm rail, draw a chalk line from the edge of the fabric ending in a small Y-shape 1½ in. (4 cm) short of the side. Cut the lines.

7(b) Push the rear section of fabric down in between the arm rail and the seat pad.

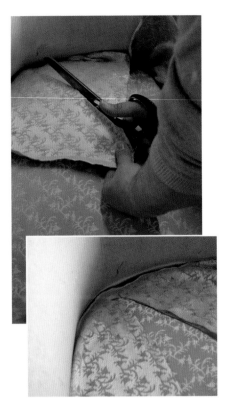

7(c) Pull the fabric through to the outside. Now repeat on the other side.

7(e) Push the two sections of fabric down either side of the rail.

7(d) On the diagonal, make a Y-shaped cut to the back rail in the same way, drawing it on with chalk first and finishing the cut short of the back.

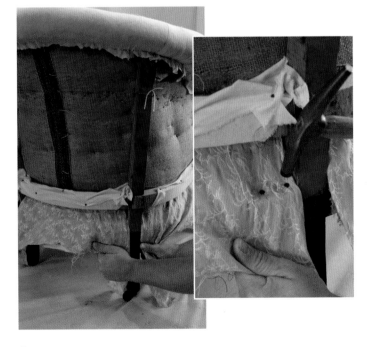

8 Pull the fabric through from the outside. Repeat on the other back corner. Pull the fabric taut and tack it to the bottom rail on the outside.

9 Tack both sides and the back of the seat cover. Your chair should now look like this.

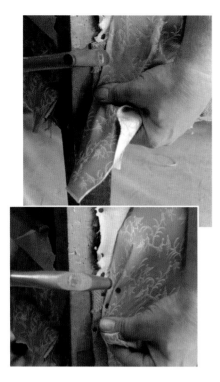

BACK MEASURING FOR THE TOP COVER

The shape of the back, which curves and slopes into the arms, is best dealt with by sewing three separate pieces of fabric together. We decided to use piping to make a feature of the seams.

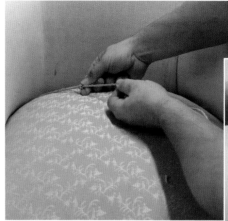

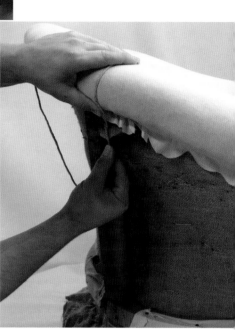

10 Work both sides. Fold the outside edge of the fabric and pull it firmly down, slightly to the side. Tack, taking in the cotton wadding and trimming if necessary. Make a pleat, as shown here, to take out fullness and then tack. Trim off any surplus fabric.

11 The simplest way to measure your fabric is to mark the seam points with Italian hemp twine. Tie the Italian hemp twine to the leg with a slip knot (see page 15). Push it through to the front and take it up over the top. Tack in position. We decide to make our seams just to the front of the back uprights.

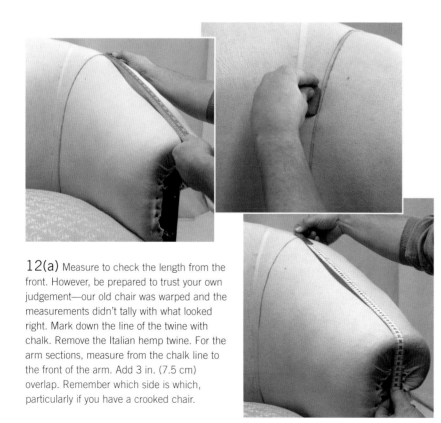

12(a) Measure to check the length from the front. However, be prepared to trust your own judgement—our old chair was warped and the measurements didn't tally with what looked right. Mark down the line of the twine with chalk. Remove the Italian hemp twine. For the arm sections, measure from the chalk line to the front of the arm. Add 3 in. (7.5 cm) overlap. Remember which side is which, particularly if you have a crooked chair.

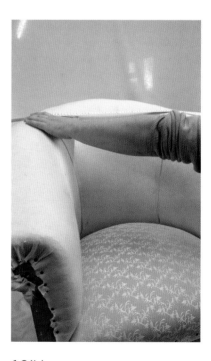

12(b) For the back, measure between the chalk lines adding 3 in. (7.5 cm) either side to allow for the flex around the curve. Measure the top-cover fabric and cut out.

CUTTING THE TOP COVER

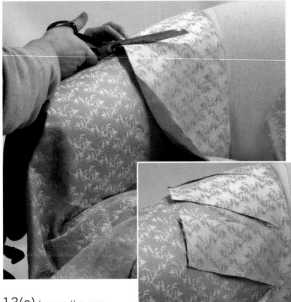

13(a) Lay on the arm piece, folding it over so that the fold lies along the chalk line. Inset: Cut into the fabric as shown, finishing the cut 1½ in. (4 cm) from the fold.

13(b) Repeat on the other side.

14(a) Repeat on the back, folding the fabric to butt up to the arm fold and snipping into the fabric on both seam folds. Pin each side of the seams into place.

14(b) Using tailor's chalk, mark out a ½-in. (1.25-cm) seam allowance either side of both seams.

15(a) Trim the seams along the chalk marks.

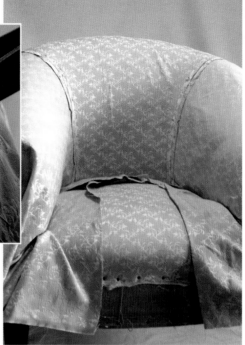

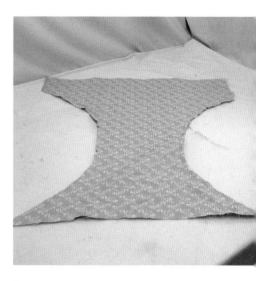

15(b) Cut a notch either side of the seams every 4 in. (10 cm), so that you can line up the fabric when you stitch it.

16 Take out the pins and remove the fabric for sewing. The sides will have a notched curve at one end. The back piece will look like the photo above. (Note that it looks slightly uneven. This is because of the warping of our chair.)

STITCHING THE TOP COVER

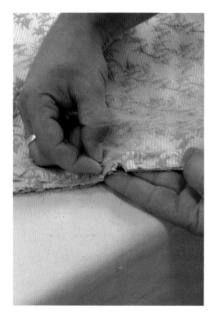

17 Make single piping with a ½-in. (1.25-cm) raw edge to match the seam allowance on your fabric (see page 137). Pin and machine stitch the piping onto the curved edges of the back section.

18(a) With right sides together, matching the notches, stitch the curved edges of the arm sections to the back's piped edges.

18(b) This results in an apparently ungainly arrangement of fabric.

LAYING ON COTTON FELT AND COTTON WADDING

19 Lay on the cotton felt, one piece for the back and one each for the sides. Tear and knit together with your hands, pushing the edges down the sides of the seat, as shown.

20 Again in three pieces, lay on a double layer of cotton wadding, tucking down the sides and tacking sparingly to just under the top roll.

FITTING THE TOP COVER

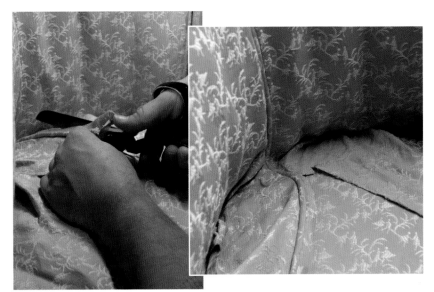

21 Position the top cover. Make a temporary tack in the center of the top back rail and temporary tack out to the piping. Tuck in the lower edge to make the cover taut, without tucking in the raw edges. Make Y-cuts on the back side of the piping to fit the cover around the back uprights. The cuts should line up with the cuts you made in the seat cover. Tug the ends through to the outside. At this point, it is worth adjusting the temporary tacks at the back, stretching the fabric sideways to get rid of any wrinkles on the back.

22(a) Move to the arms. Temporary tack, pulling the fabric across the arm. Make Y-shaped cuts to tuck the fabric around the front uprights.

FITTING THE FABRIC AROUND THE SCROLL

The scrolls, front border and piping can be worked exactly as the day bed (page 124). We also demonstrate an optional variation using a Y-cut and folding a flap of fabric around the front of the scroll.

22(b) Temporary tack the fabric over at the top of the arms, stretching and pulling to make a snug fit. On the back and sides, tack the pulled-through flaps onto the bottom rail. Stretch and pull down the fabric as you tack.

23(a) Temporary tack the arm cover at the front before pleating.

23(b) Start pleating, as for the day bed (see page 128).

23(c) An optional variation is to make a Y-cut on the outside of the arm.

24(a) Trim the surplus fabric on the scroll. Pull the side flap across the scroll and tack.

24(b) Trim off any surplus fabric.

MAKING THE PIPED FRONT BORDER

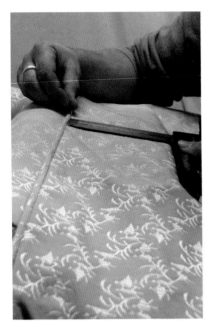

25(a) Sew a piped front border as for the Edwardian recliner (see page 119), allowing an extra 3 in. (7.5 cm) to tack under the bottom rail. Pin the border over the tack line, using the sliding bevel or a ruler to keep it straight. Slipstitch in place.

25(b) Cut two double layers of cotton wadding to fit under the border and use a few tacks to fix it in position. Pull down the border and temporary tack under the bottom rail.

25(c) Pull gently sideways until the border is smooth. Tack down the front of the uprights.

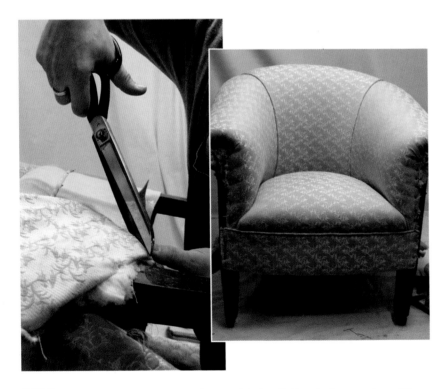

25(d) Make a straight, diagonal cut to fit around the leg. Fold under the raw edges of the border and tack under the bottom rail.

26 Trim all the pulled-through flaps and tack them up out of the way in preparation for fitting the outside back panels.

OUTSIDE BACK AND ARM PANELS MEASURING AND CUTTING THE FABRIC

The outside panels are made using the same principles as the nursing chair (page 102) but in three sections—two arm pieces and the back.

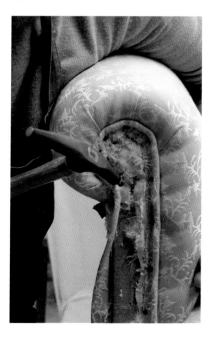

27 Make the scroll piping and facing in the same way as for the day bed (see page 129), but take the piping down over the border to the top of the leg and back up, as shown.

28 Measure and cut the panels to size, allowing an extra 3–1 in. (7.5–2.5 cm) for folding under to slipstitch and 2 in. (5 cm) to tack under the bottom.
   Starting with the arms, pin the front and top edges into position, and temporary tack the back and lower edges. Slipstitch to the side of the scroll and to the top roll, and tack the back edge to the back upright. Tack the lower edges under the bottom.
   Fit the back, pinning the sides to the arm panels and the top edge to the top roll, and temporary tack underneath. Slipstitch and tack in place.

BOTTOM CLOTH
29 Finish by attaching the bottom cloth (see page 35).

Index

Suppliers

Fabrics for Canterbury
Albert House
14 St Johns Lane
Castle St
Canterbury
Kent CT1 2QG
Tel: +44 (0)1227 457555
Fax: +44 (0)1227 457222
fabricsincant@aol.com
www.fabricsincanterbury.com

Gordon Larkin
9b Best Lane
Canterbury
Kent CT1 2JB
Tel: +44 (0)1227 454773
gordon_larkin@btconnect.com

Cabbages and Roses
5 Langton St
London SW10 0JL
Tel: +44 (0)20 7352 7333
Fax: +44 (0)20 8878 4952
enquiries@cabbagesand-
roses.com
www.cabbagesandroses.com

Jane Churchill at Colefax
and Fowler
979 Third Avenue
New York NY 10022
Tel: (001) 212-753-4488
www.janechurchill.com

Osborne and Little Inc.
90 Commerce Road
Stamford CT 06902
Tel: (001) 203-359-1500
www.osborneandlittle.com